MEXICO

Scala Books, New York

distributed by Harper & Row, Publishers

MEXICO

Photographs by Albano Guatti
Text by Antonio Haas

Design by Armando Milani

Library of Congress
Catalog Card Number
82-061170

First published
in the U.S. and Canada 1982 by
Scala Books, New York

ISBN 0-935748-47-4

Project Director
Maria Teresa Train

Consultant
Nebojša Tomašević

Edition Editors
Michael Rose
Thekla Clark

Production
Fried Rosenstock

Produced by Scala

All photographs are by Albano Guatti
except: 2, 3, 124 by *Christian Schlaepfer*,
34, 39, 112, 173 by *Albert Moldvay*, 35,
36, 49, 50, 51 by *Rogelio Cuellar*, 42, 174,
175 by *Nicolas Sapieha*, 121 by *SEF*.

Albano Guatti wishes to thank the
following: Beatriz Braniff, Teresa Pomar,
Centro Coordinador Tzeltal-Tzotzil (San
Cristobal de Las Casas), Cannon USA and
Cannon, Italia.

The author would like to express his
gratitude to the following, who were
consulted with regard to the technical
points in their specific fields of expertise.
In alphabetical order:
Pedro Aspe (the Colonial period)
Ignacio Bernal (the pre-Hispanic period)
Ricardo Elizondo (Nuevo León)
Mauricio González de la Garza (Tamaulipas)
Iñigo Laviada (the Yucatán peninsula,
Tabasco and Veracruz)
Margarita Michelena (the Federal District)
Marita Martínez del Río de Rado
(Chapultepec and the palaces of the DF)
Alejandro Rangel Hidalgo (Colima)
María Teresa Redo de Sanchez Navarro (the
pulque haciendas)
Gutiérrez Tibon (a critical reading of the
text). The above should not be held
responsible, however, for opinions
expressed in the text, nor blamed for
inaccuracies, which are all the
author's own.

Printed in Milan, Italy by
Amilcare Pizzi Arti Grafiche, S.p.A.
for Scala Books
342 Madison Avenue
New York, N.Y. 10020

Jacket illustrations:
Front: Beribboned headdress of a Puebla
dancer.
Back: 1. Chichén-Itza, pre-Hispanic
Toltec-Maya.
2. Madonna from Convent Church of
Santo Domingo, Oaxaca, Colonial period.
3. Casa Gilardi by Luis Barragán,
contemporary.

Black and white illustrations:
Preface and Chapter 1: The Florentine
Codex, Biblioteca Nazionale, Florence
and the Madrid Codex, Museo de
América, Madrid.
Chapters 2 and 4: Ancient Mexican
seals.
Chapters 3 and 5: Engravings by José
Guadalupe Posada.

MEXICO

0 ——————— 500 km

© SERVIZIO CARTOGRAFICO DEL TOURING CLUB ITALIANO, MILANO-1982-PRINTED IN ITALY

1. A colossal monolithic Olmec head, representative of the mother culture of Mesoamerica. The Olmec culture was the first of those opulent and various pre-Hispanic civilizations that ended with the Aztecs.

2. This giant plant is a maguey or pulque agave. Usually the juice is extracted and the plant cut back before it reaches this size since it only flowers once and then dies. Pulque, the drink made from the fermented juice of the maguey, was at one point the national drink of Mexico. Highly intoxicating, its use in pre-Hispanic societies was strictly prohibited except under certain special circumstances. Men over sixty and pregnant woman were allowed to drink all they wished. Drunkenness, however, was a capital offense in men under sixty and conviction for the third time carried the death sentence for the man and his entire family.

3. The tenochti, *the wild red prickly pear that gave its name to the Aztec capital of Tenochtitlán and now appears on the Mexican national flag, supporting the eagle and the serpent. This is the ultimate symbol of the sun-worshiping Aztecs for whom the eagle represented the sun and the red prickly pears the human hearts on which it fed.*

4. Near Tuxtla Gutiérrez (Chiapas). The canyon of Sumidero, said to be the place where the defending Indian troops committed collective suicide on the arrival of the conquistadors.

2

3

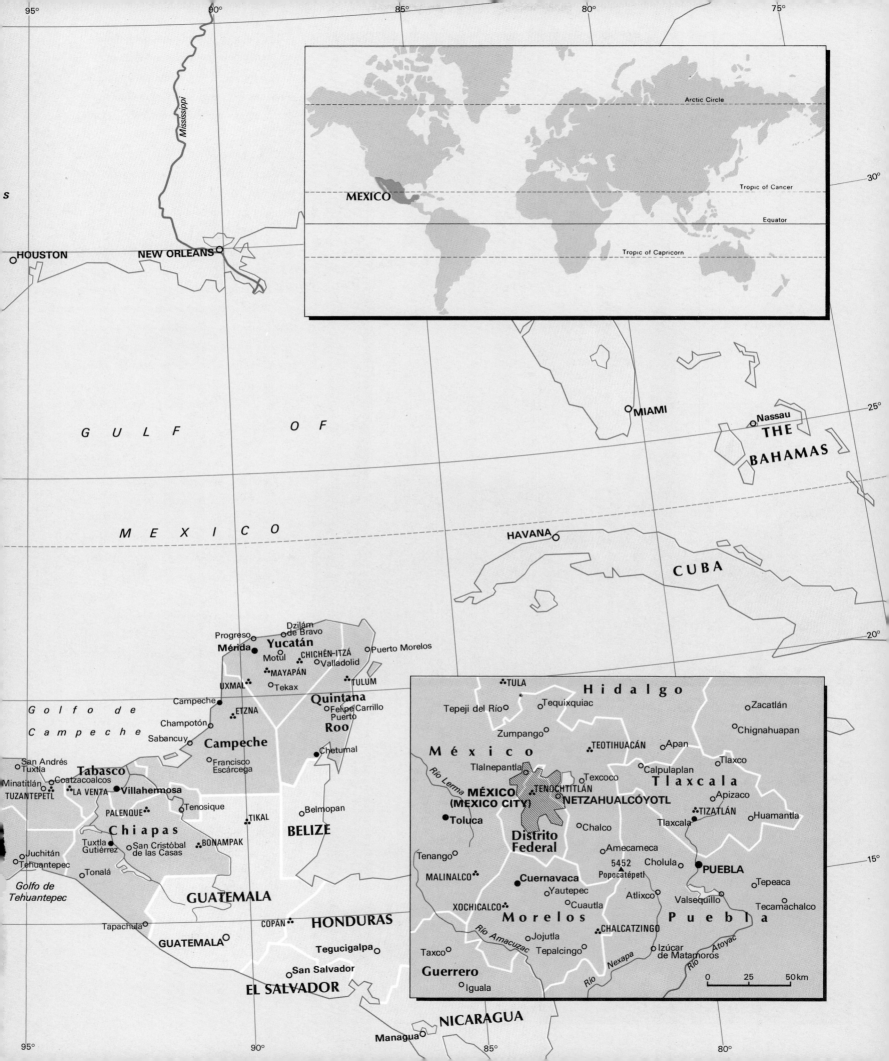

5

5. *Mexico City. The pre-Hispanic and modern architecture join hands in the Plaza de las Tres Culturas.*

6. *Huactzingo (Tlaxcala). Row of colonial-style painted houses put to modern use.*

7. *Tula (Hidalgo). Four Atlantes stand guard on top of the pyramid. They represent the god Quetzalcóatl in his capacity as "Morning Star."*

8. *Near Champoton (Campeche). Peasant paying his respects at a roadside shrine.*

5. *Mexico City. The pre-Hispanic and modern architecture join hands in the Plaza de las Tres Culturas.*

6. *Huactzingo (Tlaxcala). Row of colonial-style painted houses put to modern use.*

7. *Tula (Hidalgo). Four Atlantes stand guard on top of the pyramid. They represent the god Quetzalcóatl in his capacity as "Morning Star."*

8. *Near Champoton (Campeche). Peasant paying his respects at a roadside shrine.*

6

7

6

7

9. Sabancuy (Campeche). Painting a wall.
Sabancuy is in a countryside made lovely by
numerous lakes, the home of great numbers of
aquatic birds. Near Sabancuy is a lagoon whose
waters at the shore are of a striking blood-red
color.

10. Huistan (Chiapas). Village street scene.

11. Pinotepa Nacional (Oaxaca). Group of
men in the doorway of a bar. The painted red
bands on the wall of the building are a typical
Mexican motif.

12

12. *San Cristóbal de Las Casas (Chiapas).*

Table of Contents

Politics, Pyramids and People

The image most foreigners have of Mexico is like a sculpture by Henry Moore, strong and expressive but full of holes. It is the result of much tampering with the facts by political chroniclers who view history as an inexhaustible mine of source material which they can mold to their own purposes.

The first big void that needs filling in spans most of our archeological past *before* the Aztecs. In that "dark backward and abysm of time" there flourished opulent and various cultures whose names mean little or nothing today, so the word "Aztec" has therefore become a generic term for everything that existed before the Spaniards. Thus an Air France captain, on a flight out of Mexico City, can point out the "Aztec" pyramids of Teotihuacán, which is like calling the Pyramids of Gizeh "Islamic", and even a writer as knowledgeable as Lincoln Kirstein has referred to one of the Toltec Chac-Mool reclining figures as an "Aztec God."

The Spanish Conquest itself, on the other hand is so vividly remembered that it needs little special attention: there are novels and studies galore on that extraordinary exploit. But after the fall of the Aztec capital in 1521, there is another gap of centuries before the familiar 1860's tableau of that famous *mano a mano* between the Hapsburg Emperor Maximilian and Benito Juárez, the Zapotec Indian who defeated him. (Brian Aherne and Paul Muni, to those who remember the thirties, with Bette Davies playing the mad Empress Carlota to the hilt). Yet this black hole in our knowledge conceals the very centuries in which the Mexican nation developed its own particular character and began to play its historical role.

After this Mexico blacks out for another fifty years until images of the 1910 Revolution suddenly appear on the scene (Marlon Brando now plays Zapata, Wallace Beery is Pancho Villa). They yell and shake their fists a while, and then at last history fades away to be replaced by the silken beaches and glossy hotels of Acapulco, Vallarta and Cancún.

The foregoing is not an idle joke. It is, in fact, uncomfortably close to the truth. An astonishing number of well-read foreigners, even among our closest neighbors, know little more than this about Mexico. The object of the present book, then, is to briefly reconstruct our history and establish a certain continuity between these scattered episodes. We lack the space here for the complete job which the subject really needs, but we will at least try to fill out the Henry Moore image with texts and pictures, and so present Mexico as a whole rather than a series of holes.

Visions and Revisions

History is invariably written by the winner, and Mexico gets periodically reinvented at least once after each major upheaval. In Aztec times, Itzcóatl burned the books to suit his needs, so the intent and extent of later editorial revisions, including that of the Spaniards' with respect to the Aztecs, should not surprise us.

The War of Independence (1810-21), the Mexican-American War (1846-47), the anti-clerical Reform Laws and the Constitution of 1857, all produced radical switches in historical opinion. Maximilian's Empire and the French Intervention (1864-67) brought lasting discredit to the Conservatives who had tricked the guileless Archduke into believing that the Mexican people yearned for their old Austrian monarchs (an idea that probably didn't sound as crazy then as it does now). But after Juárez came Porfirio Díaz, who ran for the Presidency on a platform of no re-election and then proceeded to re-elect himself for seven consecutive terms. This time, of course, the Conservative historians had a field day at the expense of the Liberals.

Don Porfirio cleared the countryside of its native bandits, while bringing in foreign experts to drag it reluctantly into the Industrial Age. He was fairly successful, but he did not measure the social and political cost and his reign ended in the Revolution of 1910. (This is *the* Revolution in Mexico, always with a capital R.) Nevertheless, he was the only President who left more money in the till than was in it when he took over. Revolutionary historians are all too often rampant revisionists. They have deified Juárez at the expense of Díaz, whose colossal administrative achievements are to this day passionately ignored.

After our eleven-year struggle for Independence, the United States emerged as our staunchest ally against Spain. The Mexican-American War, however, soon revealed the nature of this friendship. The loss of over half Mexico's territory — Texas and everything between it and the Pacific coast, right up through California to Oregon — led to the general feeling that it was "the patriotic duty of every Mexican to consider the United States Mexico's worst enemy." Yet twenty years later, Juárez and his liberals, grateful for American aid against the French, again looked on the United States as a loyal friend. After the Revolution, however, the villainous complicity of the American Ambassador, Henry Lane Wilson, in the assassination of President Madero, followed by the 1914 landings of the Marines in Tampico and Veracruz, definitely confirmed the United States as the official villain in Mexico's books.

For this reason, most Mexicans were *germanofilos* during World War II. Hitler became our unintended champion against the *gringo* — a sixteenth-century word, incidentally, (that has nothing to do with any soldier's song about "Green grow the rushes, O!") that is merely a corruption of *griego*, "Greek," which became a generic Spanish term for any foreign trader.

Anti-yanqui feeling, however, has never stopped prosperous Mexicans from sending their offspring to American schools, their aches and pains to the Mayo Clinic (or, nowadays, Houston) and their savings to New York. Nor has it stopped the millions who cannot afford even the bare necessities of existence from taking the risk of crossing the United States border, in search of work and the kind of security unattainable in their native land. So clearly, a large gap opens between the official view of the "Colossus of the North" and what the neediest of our people really think about it.

The Two Sides of the Family

Our attitude toward Spain is also one of violent ambivalence. Spain is the country to which we owe our supreme cultural debt, yet with which we still seem to be fighting for our independence. We have never cut the umbilical cord. Spain has become the country we love to hate — after the United States, that is — and, also, after the United States, the country we most like to visit.

In one of the Diego Rivera murals in the National Palace there is a list headed Mexico's "Contributions to the world:" maize, chocolate, avocadoes, tomatoes, chili peppers, among other things, which identifies the modern country with the pre-Hispanic land. This is the official line. Aside from the fact that the list includes nothing man-made or of social significance, its supporters would do well to remember what Spain brought to us: draft animals, horses, cattle, wheat, citrus fruits, bananas, sugar cane, the *wheel* — not to mention wine, Christianity and the Spanish language. Even the Virgin of Guadalupe was imported from Spain (she presented herself miraculously and of her own volition to the Indian Juan Diego).

Why Mexico finds it so difficult to accept the immensity of her debt to Spain is an enigma. Admittedly, our archeological past is infinitely more beguiling to intellectuals and tourists than the monuments of the colonial period; magnificent as these may be they are hardly as original as the Plumed Serpent, the deified Quetzalcóatl, or the serpent-kirtled Coatlicue. But the fact remains that fully 90% of the population consists of Spanish-speaking Catholics, so even our rejection of Spain is couched in the language she gave us, and even our atheists deny the existence not of Huitzilpochtli but of the Christian God. And as a crowning absurdity, we call Spain "*la Madre Patria*," "the Mother Fatherland."

In the end we have to agree with the early Spaniards that the original natives were just not very practical. A workable wheel appears in some of their toys, for instance, yet it never occurred to them to give it real work to do. The Aztecs worshiped an image of Huitzilpochtli made of cornmeal paste – they had, in other words, an edible god before them – but instead of taking the further step of consuming him eucharistically, as the Christians did, they continued to allow him to eat them. They lacked the imagination to effect a symbolic substitution of the kind mythographically represented by the captive ram Jehovah sent to Abraham in Isaac's place. Human sacrifice showed no sign of abating at the time of the Spaniards' arrival. Its overt purpose was to keep the celestial mechanics in working order, for the Indians believed that without an abundant supply of human blood the sun would refuse to rise the following morning.

Mexico's attitude toward Hernán Cortés again reflects our ambivalence toward Spain. A Salamanca law school drop-out, he was beyond doubt the greatest of the conquistadors. In dealing with the natives he showed himself a matchless politician as well as a brave and crafty warrior: he was a settler and a lawgiver, not a hit-and-run exploiter. An advocate of Spanish-Indian intermarriage, he practically invented, by enthusiastic personal example, the *Mestizo*, Christian, Spanish-speaking Mexican people of today.

To many Mexicans, Cortés is still the one unquestionable hero of our history, the true founder of our nationality. Yet officially, especially since the Revolution, his name has been practically expunged from the records. There is no official memorial to him in the country he so imaginatively helped to create. Cuauhtémoc, on the other hand, the last of the Aztec emperors and Cortés's defeated foe, has become a national hero, perhaps *the* national hero. Such martyr-worship seems neurotic: even his name, symbolic of the setting sun, suggests defeat. Yet cities, towns and countries – even a brewery – are named after him, and his admirers gather once a year to celebrate his glory in a language he abominated.

The Spanish Conquest has thus been turned into a reverse western. The Indians are the heroes, the conquistadors are the villains (with Moctezuma II in between, wandering about like Hamlet in the wrong play, half persuaded that Cortés was the returning Quetzalcóatl). Yet we know that many natives preferred the Spaniards to their Aztec overlords, so much so that they formed the bulk of Cortés's conquering troops, thus proving the truth of the old aphorism that the Conquest of Mexico was achieved by the Indians, and not the conquistadors, a fact frequently and deliberately overlooked.

We also know that the Aztec empire covered less than twenty per cent of Mexico's present territory, yet the official premise is that anything Aztec is more authentically "Mexican" than anything contributed by the Spaniards who created Mexico, when they brought the Aztecs and the other conquered tribes and territories into the mainstream of European culture. Yet even now any successful athletic team is proudly referred to as "the Aztec contingent," while Cortés is called "*our* first invader," as if Mexico were an Indian country. Even the Aztec Cuauhtémoc is venerated as the great "Mexican" hero!

The truth of the matter is that the Aztecs were *Mexicas* (mesh-*chic*-as), not Mexicans. Mexican is a term that evolved slowly and did not come into common use until well into the eighteenth century. We did not legally become Mexicans until after

our break with Spain in 1810, with the creation of the first Mexican republic. As one of our writers put it: "*Yo soy mexicano, mexica, no!*"

Though we are neither Mexicas nor Spaniards, we are clearly heirs to both, and some distinctive indigenous elements have survived alongside the Spanish in modern Mexican life and manners. Our diet, for example, is probably the one thing Cuauhtémoc would recognize: maize tortillas, chili peppers, a bounty of fruits and vegetables, some game and plenty of red meat (though not from any livestock he would have known). And the poorer, meatless diet of our Indian peasant probably differs little from that of his historical counterpart, the Aztec *macehual*.

Our vocabulary is another case in point. Mexican Spanish is so interlarded with words from the vernaculars, especially Náhuatl, that several massive dictionaries of *mexicanismos* have been compiled. In the Yucatán area, Mayan is still the lingua franca, and there are old gentlemen around who, having spent their school years in France, still count in French, argue in Spanish and lapse into Mayan about the house. As a general rule, the homier the topic, the further Mexican speech veers from standard Spanish into Spaztec or whatever, and beyond a certain point, our speech inevitably sounds more Indian than Spanish to a Spaniard's ear.

By the same token, the Spaniard strikes us as being unnecessarily brusque both in his speech and manner, from which it seems reasonable to assume that the peculiar Mexican circumspection, at once so mannerly and so noncommittal that it can be interpreted equally as timidity, deviousness, or simply the most exquisite courtesy, has come from our Indian roots. This trait is stronger in southern Mexicans than in northerners, but in either case, forthrightness is not our forte.

Certain institutions have survived in Mexico that were common to both Mesoamerica and feudal Spain. Of these, the most important is the *ejido*, a system of common land tenure based on a right to the land and production, that is usufruct rather than outright ownership. No understanding of twentieth-century Mexico is possible without a close look at that institution.

In the Aztec state, the communal lands were called *calpulalli*. Although they were inalienable, the right to farm them was individual and could be handed down from father to son. In Spain, the ejido was the village common, which in the walled towns lay immediately outside the exit gate. Hence the term *exido* (modern spelling, ejido), which Gongora sang in his *Soledados*:

> *Y qual mancebos texen anudados*
> *Feftivos choros en alegre exido . . .*

which rather untranslatably refers to the lads singing glees on the common. The Mexican ejido, then, has clear antecedents on both sides of the family. It is more a revival than a survival, however, since all corporate land, including the Indian *comunidades*, were outlawed by the 1857 Constitution. In their attempt to liquidate and put into circulation the immense wealth held in mortmain by the church, the Reform Laws turned the *comuneros* into small landowners. Unaccustomed to private ownership, they soon sold or mortgaged, and lost their land to the neighboring *hacendados*, who thus built up their *haciendas* into vast estates while the Indians were reduced to hiring themselves out as *peons* on what used to be their own land. (Juárez's responsibility in the break up of the comunidades, incidentally, is seldom, if ever, mentioned). This tragic imbalance of property triggered the peasants' revolt led by Zapata, which in time became the mainstream of the 1910 Revolution and the *raison d'être* for the Agrarian Reform that defined the limits and conditions of land tenure.

The mechanization of agriculture has turned most of these limitations into obstacles. Production is lagging. Bound to the land like feudal serfs, *ejidatarios* by the millions are abandoning the land for the cities or (illegally) entering into the U.S. Yet despite its manifest failure, the ejido is held sacrosanct, and any proposal to eliminate it is shouted down as counter-revolutionary and anti-patriotic. The ruling party has blithely sacrificed the ejidatario to preserve the ejido. The motive was neatly stated by a former Secretary of Agriculture: "The ejido has been organized to vote, not to produce." The ruling party cannot afford to let it disappear: it is the ultimate self-perpetuating voting machine.

Our crushing centralism is another survival from our double-rooted past. It is the product of two absolute monarchies, the Spanish and the Aztec, merging into one under the equally central aegis of the Roman Catholic Church. In the nineteenth century, the decision of independent Mexico to finally turn itself into a Federal Republic had little practical effect: it did not actually do much to decentralize the country, nor did it make logical or historical sense. From the first, Mexico was not a group of mutually independent entities like the thirteen American colonies, but a single centralized state. As a result, our federalism has never been more than a formality which has in no way reduced the power of the president. There is a macabre footnote to this: the vice-presidency does not exist in Mexico. It was eliminated in 1847 as being too hazardous to the president's health and thus to the stability of the country. Though it was restored late in don Porfirio's reign, it again disappeared with the Revolution, and has never been re-instated. Mexico, in sum, is the offshoot of two rich and powerful civilizations, empires, in fact, which had in common numerous social and political institutions. Many of these have survived. The difference between the two empires, however, are even more numerous, and a brief look around shows that these, too, have continued into the present day.

Vestiges of Mesoamerica are all about us, undigested and, perhaps, undigestible. The ruins of this civilization are what most travelers want to see when they visit Mexico. Though they stand on Mexican territory, they are not in any other sense Mexican but in reality Mesoamerican, whether they be Olmec, Teotihuacán, Zapotec, Mayan, Toltec or Aztec.

The surviving Indians are, however, indisputably Mexican. Millions still live in their cultural fastnesses, practicing their shamanistic cults with psychotropic drugs, such as the "god's flesh" mushroom of Oaxaca in the south and the *peyote* in the north. Some, like the Lacandones and the Seris, who appeared to be doomed to extinction are now actually beginning to multiply again.

The city Indians, on the other hand, are lamentably *au courant* in both material and intellectual fashions. The students among them fill the air with Marxist static; the mystics seek Nirvanas; while the hedonists grab at every fad with a U.S. label. They are, in other words, exactly like their Creole and Mestizo counterparts. But it must be admitted that alienation among them takes some singularly unprepossessing forms – which in any case only succeed in doing what foreign fashions generally do: revealing what their wearers are trying hardest to conceal. Nothing has replaced the ties that once bound them to their ancient dignities. Neither the U.S. nor the USSR can help them, neither communism nor consumerism. Only – perhaps – a search for the lasting values of Mexico.

Before Cortés

To help the reader in what follows, a rough guide is provided at the back of the book, with glossaries and chronological tables containing basic information.

The Olmecs (1200-300 BC)

In order to fill in the pre-Aztec void, the colossal Olmec heads of Tabasco and southern Veracruz make a good starting point. Single blocks of basalt weighing as much as thirty tons sculpted by masters, they were found resting pensively on the soft alluvial floor of a rain forest, and in the soil of a swampy island, leagues away from the closest stone quarry. Without the wheel, how did they get there? Without iron tools, how did they come into being?

We know very little about the Olmecs. Even the name is a later Náhuatl designation, meaning "dweller of the rubber country." They did, however, create what is known as "the mother culture" of Mesoamerica, since it provided the basic crafts and techniques for all subsequent cultures. It is now generally believed that it was the Olmecs, and not the Maya, who invented the zero as a mathematical concept. Their culture dominated the period between 1200 and 300 BC or, to put it in European terms, between the fall of Crete and the death of Alexander the Great. It was followed by the Classical period, which corresponds roughly to the first millenium of the Christian era, during which time three great cultures flowered simultaneously in Mesoamerica: the Mayan in the Yucatán peninsula; the Monte Albán Zapotec in Oaxaca; and, in the high central plateau near what is now Mexico City, the culture associated with the sacred city of Teotihuacán.

Teotihuacán (100-900 AD)

This greatest of pre-Hispanic city-states had a definitive influence on all later developments in Mexico. Its grandeur was unsurpassed. Giants were supposed to have built it, their huge buried bones filling everyone with astonishment (as well they might, since they belonged to extinct mammoths). Teotihuacán was the first true city to develop alongside a ceremonial center. At its height, with almost 200,000 inhabitants, it may well have been the most populous city in the world.

The Aztecs, coming upon its ruins, called it "the City of the Gods," which is what Teotihuacán means (the root word *teo*, by a curious phonetic coincidence, meaning "god" in Náhuatl as well as in various Indo-European languages). Pilgrims came to worship there from the furthest corners of Mesoamerica, and took home its merchandise, its crafts and styles. Moctezuma himself made occasional pilgrimages to Teotihuacán. He had a special devotion for Quetzalcóatl, the Plumed Serpent, whose prediction of his own second coming so fatally weakened Moctezuma before Cortés.

Some time between 650 and 700, Teotihuacán was sacked and put to the torch by unknown invaders. It never recovered. The old population emigrated, founding new cities. Foreign peoples arrived and settled among the ruins. And following the twilight of Teotihuacán, the classic Maya and Monte Albán cultures also began to decay. The sack of Teotihuacán and the later plundering of Tula, the Toltec capital, show that native conquerors were every bit as destructive as the Spaniards were to be. Conquerors, after all, come to impose themselves, and what they do not raze to the ground they use as building blocks for their own memorials.

The Toltecs (900-1300 AD)

The southward migration of peoples never seemed to stop. Always pressing down from the north were the barbarous nomadic tribes known generically as "*Chichimecas*," literally "sons of bitches," a totemic designation which, not having yet acquired its current affectionate overtones, was almost certainly intended as an insult by people of the established cultures.

Like all "new" tribes, the Toltecs came south from Chichimec country (though the chronicler Torquemada in the eighteenth century suggested that they were descended from the Irish). They soon established themselves in the rich central valleys and made Culhuacan, near Xochimilco, their capital. They adopted the cult of the Plumed Serpent from Teotihuacán and in time passed it on to the Aztecs.

The worship of Quetzalcóatl was a key element in the development of the

Toltecs. Quetzalcóatl was already a deity and was later, as a historical man, an inspired leader who lived around the year 1000, adopted the deity's name and came to be considered his pontiff or even his messiah. The historic Quetzalcóatl moved the Toltec capital north from Culhuacan to Tollan, later known as Tula, which became the seat of Toltec power.

The mythical Quetzalcóatl that issued from the merging of man and deity was of supreme importance in pre-Hispanic lore. Historically, he was a civilizer, credited with the invention of writing and the development of the agricultural arts. His pacifism was his undoing. Priests of a bloodier cult ousted him and his followers, who migrated south to Cholula and eventually ended up in Chichén Itzá, a modest Mayan outpost which they converted into the impressive city whose ruins we know.

Tradition has dealt kindly with Quetzalcóatl. It has metamorphosed him into a monotheistic messiah who stood firmly against human sacrifice. At the end of his life he is said to have built a raft and sailed off toward the eastern sky, promising to return on the year whose number he bore as his given name. To Moctezuma's misfortune, this number coincided precisely with the year in which Cortés landed on the eastern shores of his empire.

The Mexica-Aztecs (1325-1521)

The prestige of the Toltecs continued to grow even after the fall of Tula. Though the name, "place of rushes (*tules*)" was originally a metaphor for any populous city, when applied to Tollan it came to mean "City of peace and bliss," something like the New Jerusalem of Christian thought. The Toltecs were the great people of the past, and to be descended from them conferred instant aristocracy. The Mexicas grasped at once the significance of Toltec status, and as they rose to power, they sought legitimacy by marrying into the ruling family of Culhuacan. Even Moctezuma married a lady from Tula, and, after the Conquest, his son, don Pedro, was made Governor, while *his* descendants in Spain are now Dukes of Moctezuma de Tultengo.

A pilgrim tribe from the Chichimec north, the Mexicas had come south many years earlier in search of their promised land, which would be marked for them by a cactus on which they would see an eagle devouring a serpent (a curious mythographic separation of the Plumed Serpent into its component bird and reptile elements). The sign appeared on a rocky island in the middle of (the then enormous) Lake Texcoco, and there they founded the city they called Tenochtitlán, "place of the wild prickly pear."

Eventually Tenochtitlán became the capital of the largest empire Mesoamerica was ever to know. By that time, waging war with their neighbors had become the Aztecs' way of life. They fought not only for loot and tribute but also to satisfy their gods' increasing demand for human blood. This made them hugely unpopular overlords, so when Cortés arrived, the subject peoples were ready to pull away and the independent lords only too willing to help a likely challenger.

The Conquest

Cortés was always lucky in his timing. He dropped out of Salamanca in time to take part in the conquest of Cuba. Put in charge of an expedition to the Mexican mainland and correctly suspecting a plot to replace him, he shipped out before the appointed time. Once on shore he felt himself threatened so he summoned his officers and created the municipality of Veracruz just in time to put himself legally beyond the reach of his enraged superior. Then – unexpected bonus – he landed in 1519, which in the Aztec calendar was *Ce Acatl* (one reed) – the very year in which the mythic Quetzalcóatl had promised to return.

The news of Cortés's landing burst on the Aztec court like a nova. Who else could this be but the departed god come to reclaim his heritage: Moctezuma sent gifts of gold, turquoise and quetzal feathers, and a polite message to the effect that the Emperor was not "at home."

The rest of the story is too well known to need retelling. Gold rooted the Spaniards to the new land. Cortés, correctly reading the mood of the natives, exploited their hostility toward the Aztecs and pressed the Spanish emperor's claim right up to Moctezuma's throne. After Moctezuma's death and Cortés's temporary defeat by Cuauhtémoc, the independent city-state of Tlaxcala gave Cortés asylum and helped him to restore his forces. Without the support of the Tlaxcaltecas and about forty thousand other natives, Cortés and his straggling body of Spaniards could never have taken Tenochtitlán.

The city fell on 13 August, 1521. It took Cortés a scant two years to carry out what is known as "the Conquest of Mexico."

The Viceregency

That unfortunate phrase "the Conquest of Mexico," has been responsible for much of our traditional resentment of Spain. That "Mexico," after all, was not our Mexico. "We" were not conquered: the Aztecs were. Yet the feeling persists, after centuries of rancor and misunderstanding.

The Spaniards wanted gold and they did not hide the fact. After one look at Moctezuma's gifts – which later caused even Albrecht Dürer to exclaim in wonder – nothing could have held them back.

"My companions and I suffer from a disease of the heart which can only be cured by gold," said Cortés to Moctezuma's ambassadors, by way of excusing his refusal to leave the land. He spoke only a half truth. When gold lust is really a disease, not all the gold in the world can cure it.

Not surprisingly, then, the quest for gold was the initial force behind the colonization of New Spain. As soon as they got their bearings, the conquistadors found there was a distinct division between the settled, civilized, agricultural south, the main source of the Aztec empire's wealth, and the barren, mountainous wilderness to the north, the country of the savage, nomadic Chichimecs. So the conquistadors' first step was to take over the rich agricultural south. This they did by means of the *encomienda*, a legal trust whereby the population of whole villages and towns, or even regions, were farmed out to the Spaniards to be educated and converted in exchange for personal services. This encomienda fulfilled the Spanish Crown's agreement with Rome, by which Spain could only legitimately own the land if it undertook to convert the conquered natives and instruct them in the Christian faith.

The conquistadors turned *encomenderos* (trustees) cared nothing about their charges' souls (with the notable exception of Cortés himself). They had undertaken the Conquest at their own expense and considered the encomienda quite simply their due, so they proceeded to squeeze it for all it was worth, making it practically indistinguishable from outright slavery.

As the wealth of the Aztecs was funnelled into the treasure chests of Spain, the landscape changed, though not the lot of the native inhabitants. Instead of pyramid tombs and temples, rising out of the forest, bell towers, churches, convents now appeared. In both cases the building was done by Indian slave labor, but now at least they had iron tools and wheeled contraptions. The earliest convents functioned as schools, farms, hospitals and orphanages, and the mendicant orders that built them were the Indians' principal advocates before the Crown. They caused the 1542 New

Laws of the Indies to be promulgated, which sought to protect the natives against the most flagrant of the conquistadors' abuses though with little immediate success.

In the meantime, the search for precious metals continued and was in time richly rewarded, though not so much by gold as by the silver strikes in the badlands to the north. Prospectors braved the Chichimecs to reach their Eldorado and stake out their claims. Settlements appeared around every new mine. Merchants followed in droves and soon became bankers to the local populace. Fortunes were made and lost and prosperous communities became ghost towns in the vicinity of the principal mining centers. Trade routes opened between the mines and Mexico City. At first provisions and draft animals were still so prohibitively expensive that cattle ranches and produce farms were soon established near the mines. The Crown built roads and *presidios* (garrison towns) to protect the bullion it so desperately needed. Troops were sent to clear the land of Chichimecs, who in a single generation had become superb horsemen. And the original conquistadors, Cortés included, were shunted aside by the viceroys and the lawyers.

This clipping of wings, apart from protecting the Indians from the conquistadors' abuses, had as its principal purpose the establishment of the absolute power of the Crown. It succeeded, more or less, but three centuries later its profoundly weakening effects began to show. In the absence of incentives, no new race of conquistadors emerged to take the northern marches by brute force. For a long time the north remained almost as sparsely settled as when it had been exclusively Chichimec land, its frontiers no more than a judicial and cartographic convention. Scattered haciendas and missions, necessarily built like fortresses, did not create the kind of undisputed possession which is nine points of the law. The social fabric was totally permeable from outside. Early in the nineteenth century, pioneers from the U.S. started going west in considerable numbers. Many settled in Mexican territory. By the 1830's, they outnumbered the Mexicans in Texas and in much of California. The rest we know.

The Apostolate

Whatever the faults of the Spanish Crown, it never neglected its missionary obligations. "The spiritual conquest of Mexico" is a chapter of grace and glory. Cortés's Mercedarian chaplain, Bartolomé de Olmedo, a saintly and prudent man, always tried to temper the conquistadors' zeal to the shorn Indian lamb.

When the twelve Franciscan "apostles" arrived in 1524, Cortés astonished the natives by kneeling to kiss the hem of the friars' tattered habits. They asked if the newcomers were "like Father Bartolomé." Once reassured, they willingly accepted definitive conversion.

This took place not so much by discarding past beliefs as by the addition of new ones. "Syncretism" is the term for the process and neither the Church nor the natives were new at the game. The Aztecs had picked up many a belief in their wanderings, most notably the cult of the Plumed Serpent. Christianity simply added another layer of beliefs to their religious baggage – one, moreover, which proved remarkably easy to carry.

Certain theological concepts stumped them, however, especially those unsupported by pragmatic results. The Eucharist, for example. The idea of eating God's flesh instead of vice versa certainly provided a welcome change from Aztec practice, though it could hardly be new to Indians who ritually ate the hallucinogenic mushroom known precisely as "god's flesh": *teonanacatl*. But eating the mushroom actually produced a rush of divine power through the bloodstream, whereas the communion wafer seemed to be totally ineffective. Many Indians continued both practices "just in case ... "

The natives took more readily to the ritualistic rather than the doctrinal approach, and there the Church's genius for syncretism won the day. The missionaries had themselves been converted by their love for the Indians, for their languages and civilization, a love of their virtues and of their weaknesses which frequently led to their turning against the conquistadors in defense of the Indians. Armed with their knowledge and practicing their own brand of syncretism, the missionaries allowed their converts to preserve many of their religious practices, eliminating only human sacrifices and the gods who demanded them. Any native deity that could be fitted into the Christian pantheon soon found his niche there. Presently, a sanctuary to the dark-skinned Virgin of Guadalupe rose on the hilltop where the Indians had previously worshipped Tonantzin, their revered mother-goddess. This was the Church's greatest tactical triumph in Mexico. It both encouraged the early converts' adoration of their native deity and satisfied the Spaniards' nostalgic devotion to their own Virgin of Guadalupe in Extremadura.

The Virgin of Guadalupe is the essence of the spirit of Mexico. That is no exaggeration. During the War of Independence she was the patroness of the Insurgents (her rival, the Royalists' Virgen de los Remedios, was known as "*La gachupina*," rather like calling her a Spanish gringa). Now even atheists are devotees of hers. The painter Diego Rivera, an outspoken hardcore Communist, said she was "the sole symbol of our national unity ... There is no other in heaven or earth." A Mexican may disbelieve in God, but never in *La Virgencita de Guadalupe* – Tonantzin – Our Revered Mother.

A kind of reverse syncretism also showed up in the early days. Like their conquerors, the Indians were frequently idolaters at heart. Taking the icon for the idea, they worshiped Christ less than the crucifix. There was one particular stone cross in Morelia that the natives flocked to with great devotion. After a couple of centuries it was removed from its original site. The pedestal broke open and out tumbled dozens of Aztec idols from the hollow inside. It had originally been a receptacle for human hearts. Syncretism works both ways.

More Silver

The first stupendous silver boom that made Zacatecas the second city of New Spain petered out early in the seventeenth century. By the 1630's, very little bullion was being sent to Spain. The eighteenth century saw a second silver boom of such spectacular dimensions that, while it lasted, Mexico alone was producing two-thirds of the world's silver. This was the time when the mining millionaires and the great hacendados built those splendid palaces and churches that turned Mexico into a treasure house of Spanish Baroque architecture. Meanwhile the Enlightenment and the French Revolution had set the hearts of men on fire. Napoleon's seizure of the Spanish throne left Mexico without a legitimate monarch, and the Mexicans opted violently for independence. The Insurgency, as we call our War of Independence, began in 1810, but independence was not fully achieved until 1821. At that time, Mexican conservatives, pure-blooded Spaniards to a man, seeing Spain adopt the Cádiz Constitution, joined forces with the insurgent leaders and severed Mexico's ties with the home country. Thus history turns itself inside out: just as the Indians had helped to achieve the conquest of Mexico, the Spaniards were later the prime movers in establishing Mexico's independence from Spain. In a rather perverse way, the wheel had come full circle.

Independent Mexico

The Aztec empire lasted two centuries (1325-1521), the Spanish, exactly three (1521-1821). Our 160 years of independence have not always been well spent. The truth is that, after the beginning of the War of Independence, the country lived in a state of civil war, with the dubious breathing spell of Porfirio Díaz's thirty-year dictatorship, until Plutarco Elías Calles founded the National Revolutionary Party in 1929.

During the Insurgency, Creoles (the colonial Spaniards) fought *gachupines* (the newly arrived Spaniards), the lower clergy fought the higher clergy, brothers fought brothers. Indians bore arms in both the Insurgent and Royalist ranks. After Independence, federalists and centralists kept up a running battle till the 1857 Constitution settled for that imitation federalism that has never really worked in our implacably centralist state. All that time, Freemasons and freethinkers were attacking the Church. When they succeeded in getting it disestablished by the Reform Laws, the Freemasons proceeded to wrangle among themselves for political power.

Taking advantage of the general discord, the Catholic conservatives in 1863 offered the non-existent throne of Mexico to Maximilian, who turned out to be as liberal as Juárez, with the result that the Papal Nuncio left the country in a towering rage. The quarreling republicans buried the hatchet just long enough to get an army together in support of Juárez and the Republic. In 1867, the defeated Maximilian was shot by a firing squad outside Querétaro. His last words were "*Viva Mexico!*"

The social and political divisions have been so deep among Mexicans that even the American annexation of over half our territory did not produce a uniform reaction among Mexicans. Nor did it prevent Juárez himself and the government of the restored republic from being fervent admirers of the "Colossus of the North." To this day there are Mexicans who, outraged by government corruption, are likely to ask, "Why did they stop at the border?" The answer, of course, is that they didn't. In 1847, American troops took Mexico City with very little trouble, mainly because the various political factions were too busy squabbling among themselves to defend their country and preferred the foreign invaders to the triumph of their political rivals.

Mexico, it should be clear by now, is such a bag of contradictions that even the most thoughtful find it difficult to understand. The Revolution of 1910, which we proudly and correctly call "the first social revolution of the century" (thereby putting the Russian business firmly in its place), did not end with don Porfirio's defeat and exile. The shooting and killing and brush-fire rebellions went on until the then ex-president Calles put a stop to it in 1929 by uniting the 200 odd warring factions under a single political umbrella. The party he created is still in power. It is now called the PRI, acronym for *Partido Revolucionario Institucional*, a fantasy title which implies that it is possible to be both revolutionary and institutional at the same time. Yet despite the high-handedness of the single-party system, – (the incumbent president chooses his own successor, for example) –, and despite class differences and the social problems posed by several million unassimilated Indians, Mexico is easily the most stable country in Latin America, as well as the most respectful of civil liberties. How long it can withstand the social pressures plus its repeated economic failures is a moot question, but one which belongs to another book. Here, our job is to look at the way things are now.

The very heart of Mexico City is the vast civic space of the *Zócalo*, traditionally the site of the island where the Aztecs first saw the eagle devouring the serpent on top of the *nopal* cactus. The symbol of what they saw is still there on the Mexican flag that flies every day from the flagpole in the center of that huge square. In the north-west corner, the Cathedral and the National Palace – Church and State, heart and head of the Mexican people – sit cater-corners from one another in massive though precarious equilibrium. The Cathedral bears firmly down on the Sacred Precinct of the Aztecs, near the spot where the great Temple of Tenochtitlán once stood. The National Palace rises from the foundations of the palace of Moctezuma himself. There is no doubt who won that war.

A few blocks to the north there is a curiously quiet spot, a bell of silence in the midst of the torrential traffic and the teeming apartment blocks of modern Tlatelolco, once the twin capital of Tenochtitlán. This too is a ceremonial spot, a square of sunken turf bounded by the steps of an Aztec temple demolished 460 years ago by the soldiers of Cortés during the final battle of the Conquest. In its place now stands the primitive Franciscan church of Santiago Tlatelolco, another visible reminder of the triumph of Spanish arms and the Christian faith. To the south, beyond a strip of lawn that makes symbolic room for the intervening centuries, there rises the glass and marble tower that houses the Secretariat of Foreign Relations, our connection with the rest of the modern world. This place is called the *Plaza de las Tres Culturas*, and an inscription on a marble plaque informs us that, "On the 13th of August of 1521, heroically defended by Cuauhtémoc, Tlatelolco was taken by Cortés. It was neither a triumph nor a defeat, but the painful birth of the Mestizo people that are the Mexicans of today."

A fine sentiment, elegantly expressed and dialectically impeccable: thesis, Aztec culture; antithesis, Spanish Christianity; synthesis, modern Mexico. Unfortunately, it does not quite correspond to the facts. A satisfactory and stable synthesis has yet to be achieved. Mexico remains a house divided, a triptych of living cultures that coexist in time and place, though too often with little or no mutual contact or understanding. The "painful birth" is a work in progress: Mexico is still in labor.

13. *Near Villahermosa (Tabasco). Protestant church on the road to Coatzacoalcos.*

14. *Aquacatenango (Chiapas). Afternoon siesta. Note the fresh grass spread on the floor, often to be found at parties and other gatherings.*

15. *Tekax (Yucatán). Child in a hammock in a private house. Hammocks are very often used in place of beds in Yucatán.*

16. *Felipe Carrillo Puerto (Quintana Roo). Interior of a local restaurant.*

14

17

17. Mérida (Yucatán). Girls sitting by the wall of a house.

18. Chamula (Chiapas). Main door of a church in this Tzotzil Indian village.

19. *Progreso, near Mérida (Yucatán).*
Fishmonger chopping ice in the market at this
seaside town.

20. *Mérida (Yucatán). Hatmaker at work.*

21. *Mexico City. Chopping sugar cane in the*
market of La Merced.

19

MÉXICO

Locals call Mexico City "el DF" – short for the Federal District – though it has spilled over into the neighboring State of Mexico and is gradually encroaching on all the neighboring towns and villages in the valley. It is a sprawling megalopolis screaming for a caesarian section. It has to be delivered of the monstrous bureaucratic baby that has inflated it to bursting point. Foreigners can only conceive what it has become if they can imagine New York, Washington and Chicago all packed into the District of Columbia and surrounded by the Rockies. Unless the smokestack industries are banished from the valley and the federal government is moved far enough away to place it out of the reach of commuters, Mexico City is doomed.

This is the dismal truth. The incomparable mountain valley of Mexico – Tenochtitlán – that Alfonso Reyes once called "the air's most limpid domain," is now the biggest bowl of smog in the world. The iron-clad Spaniards who once beheld it from the pass between the snowtopped volcanoes, remembered in their old age the astonishing clarity of the air that allowed them to see from such a distance the enchanted city on the lake. And today many Mexicans, now middle-aged, can still remember the view from the opposite end when the air, like a huge lens, provided them with a panoramic vista of the snowy mountain tops, sometimes massive and clear, at other times floating in the sheer blue sky. Now their presence there has to be taken on faith alone.

The days themselves had a clearer shape then. Mornings were lofty and blue. Then, after lunch, storm clouds dragged a sudden deep dusk over the city. Rolling down Reforma or Insurgentes – you could set your watch by them – they would burst in unison over palaces and slums, drowning the geranium pots in the patio railings, flooding the narrow streets until it seemed that the primeval lake had once again reclaimed the city. They generally disappeared in time to reveal a sumptuous, slightly vulgar, sunset. Then the huge lens, washed clean, brought the night sky down to the rooftops, where lucky children got a close up of every star in the galaxy.

All that, alas, is a thing of the past, though of a remarkably recent past. The Mexican painter José Maria Velasco's matchless nineteenth-century landscapes prove that the valley had not changed much in the previous hundred years. The industrial takeoff of the fifties transformed it, turning Mexico's once crystalline penthouse of a city into a disaster area.

The facts alone are frightening. The valley of Mexico contains the D.F. plus twelve industrial municipalities pertaining to the neighboring State of Mexico. In Mexico, the word "Mexico" may refer to three different things: the country, the state or the city. To avoid confusion we will abide by the following rules. "Mexico" alone will refer to the entire country; the "State of Mexico," to the federal unit and the "DF," or "Mexico City," will refer exclusively to the capital. The DF, incidentally, was created out of a rib taken from the State of Mexico in 1824. The valley area represents a mere 0.005% of the national territory (or about 10,000 square kilometers) but lodges 17 million inhabitants, which is 25% of Mexico's total population; 50% of the country's industrial capacity is located there as well as 58% of all vehicles and 42% of the country's permanently employed work force, which receives 53% of the total wage bill. The city buys 49% of all durable consumer goods and has 60% of all the telephones. About 50% of the population consists of government employees and their dependents.

Mexico can barely hold its head up now. It has become an octopus, every arm busily scavenging and feeding the insatiable capital, which swallows up everything in sight with scant respect for our so-called federalism and our sporadic attempts at grassroots democracy. The DF is the brain, heart and belly of the entire organism.

Being both the ceremonial center and the administrative plexus of the republic, the town is always packed with petitioners, especially in the government offices. The religious center of Mexico is also there, not in the Cathedral, as one might think, but in the shrine of the Virgin of Guadalupe. This is the magnetic pole for all true Mexicans, including Marxists and practicing atheists. Every year on 12 December, the anniversary of the Virgin's apparition in 1531, pilgrims troop in from every part of the country, some advancing on their knees and wearing scapularies of spiny cactus leaves. The whole city comes to a standstill.

The failure of the agrarian reform has poured millions of peasants into the valley area, where misery at least has company and even the unemployed have a sporting chance of getting some money *somehow*. About 5 of the 17 million inhabitants live at a bare subsistence level. Their squalid shanty towns in sand pits or cheek by jowl with some of the more august residential districts, are a vivid reproach to the system.

For the bright, ambitious youngster from the provinces, with no private means to sustain him, Mexico City has traditionally been the only option. An internal brain drain toward the capital has existed since the earliest days of the republic, which led a famous female wit of the time to say "outside Mexico City, it's all Cuautitlan" – the sticks. There is reason to hope, though. The new ecological consciousness is giving these young provincials second thoughts. They are beginning to treasure the clear air and blue skies of their home towns. The risk of succumbing to galloping inertia in the provinces is far outweighed by the threat of lung cancer in the capital. Even the authorities are taking notice. After decades of allowing speculators to destroy landmarks in the city, they have now created an office to restore the buildings and protect them from further vandalism. Thanks to this official change of heart, (vigorously implemented during the López Portillo regime by the regent of the city, Carlos Hank González, as well as by the efforts of various private foundations), enough has been preserved to show why in 1803 the German traveler and polymath Alexander von Humboldt, was moved to call our capital "the City of Palaces."

Chapultepec

One spot of abiding charm is the promontory and castle of Chapultepec, which as every Mexican schoolboy knows, means "Grasshopper Hill." Four centuries ago, the hill stood on the western shore of Lake Texcoco. Until fairly recent times, it marked the western limit of the city, but now it is merely the western limit of the downtown area. The castled hilltop rises above a park of *ahuehuetes*, those aged cypresses that are the moss-bearded ancients of the Mexican forest. The park is Mexico's homage to the Bois de Boulogne. The Emperor Maximilian, who gave the castle its present appearance and devoted much attention to the grounds, had much admired the Bois on his first visit to Paris and sought to reproduce the effect here.

Like the Bois, Chapultepec is a naturally spreading expanse of woods, meadows and lakes. It is a place for children's parties, *piñatas* and toy balloons, for flying kites, impromptu soccer games and monumental museums. The most ancient artifacts can be seen in the Museum of Anthropology, the most modern – including a frail wicker op-art semblance of a Rolls-Royce – in the Rufino Tamayo Museum. (The Museum of Modern Art across the street comes a poor second in the avant-garde stakes.) The museum architecture is either masonry-impressive (Anthropology and Tamayo) or black-glass curvilinear (Modern Art). The perilously polished marble floors are their most visible trait in common.

Cars now whiz by the Reforma throughway and plunge into what were once the

shallows of Lake Texcoco and are now merely the deafening rapids of downtown traffic.

When the Mexicas first arrived in the valley, about 700 years ago, they were shunted from one place to the other by the various tribes that were already entrenched on the shore of the lake. The arrogant Toltecs of Culhuacan packed them off to a snake-infested corner of the valley, hoping that would be the end of them. The Mexicas flourished. They loved snake, and promptly ate up the entire reptile population. The Toltecs took the warning and ran the newcomers out.

They ended up in Chapultepec, harassed on all sides by their neighbors. While there, they saw the promised sign of the eagle devouring the serpent — obviously a bird after their own heart — on a little rocky island in the middle of the lake, and there they settled, thus ending their long migration from Atzlan. (From this point onwards, putting the convenience of our readers above considerations of historical accuracy, we shall call the Mexicas by their more familiar name of "Aztecs.")

After the Aztecs had married and bullied their way to power, they looked back on Chapultepec as their homeland. The later emperors liked to come back and bathe in its abundant springs. The first Moctezuma (Cortés's was the second) built an aqueduct to provide his island capital of Tenochtitlán with uncontaminated water. He had his own and his brother's name and portrait carved on the rock face of a hidden grotto. His descendants continued the custom. Moctezuma II, also called Xocoyotzin ("the younger" in Náhuatl), went further and brought trees from every corner of his empire to plant in the park, as well as fish and waterfowl to stock the lakes. This is romantically regarded as the precursor of the present Chapultepec Zoo and Botanical Garden.

The conquering Spaniards were not blind to its beauty and utility either. They built a chapel to Saint Michael on the hilltop and a country retreat for the viceroys in the park below. In 1620 a new aqueduct was built, some of whose arches are still standing on Avenida Chapultepec.

Thomas Gage, the perfidious English Dominican and apostate who left important testimony about Chiapas and Guatemala, wrote as follows about this spot in 1625:

> "I may not omit that famous place of Chapultepec, which in the heathens'
> time was the burying place of the emperors and now by the Spaniards is
> the Escorial of America, where the viceroys that die are also interred.
> There is a sumptuous palace built with many fair gardens and devices of
> water, and ponds of fish, whither the Viceroy and the gentry of Mexico
> resort for their recreation. The riches here belonging to the Viceroy's
> chapel are thought to be worth above a million crowns."

Though this sounds implausibly grander than the castle now standing, Chapultepec clearly emerges from his account as a place rich in glamour.

In the eighteenth century, two Gálvez viceroys, father and son, built a country house on the top of the hill. After many changes and additions this became the National Military Academy where the last battle of the Mexican-American war was fought on 13 September, 1847. As we know from a famous engraving of the scene, the Stars and Stripes flew above the National Palace on the following days and was still flying on 15 September, the Mexican Day of Independence.

That war, alas, is not over. It is still being fought in the hearts of Mexicans. Since earliest childhood we are told about the six youngsters, the last of the cadet corps, who died in the defense of the Castle. They are known as "the Child Heroes of Chapultepec." Every year on the anniversary of the battle in which they lost their lives, there is a brief military ceremony in their honor. During roll call, their names are added to the list of the living. As each of their names is called, a sound like a roar is heard. It is every man, woman and child present calling back, "he died for his country!"

As a young congressman from Illinois, Abraham Lincoln denounced the Mexican war in the harshest terms, and there were other American voices just as eloquent. Yet the deed was done and to the victor went the spoils, in this case — Texas having gone previously — the territory occupied by the present states of California, Arizona, New Mexico, Nevada, Utah and parts of Wyoming and Colorado. That vast territory that Mexico had freed from Spain was therefore now its neighbor's booty. (Americans wonder why their country is not universally loved in Mexico. A moment's reflection should tell them why.)

The war left the country thoroughly demoralized. The Military Academy remained a shambles until another war brought the Austrian Archduke Maximilian to Mexico. He fell instantly in love with Chapultepec and its palace and that was the end of the Military Academy. For Maximilian swiftly proceeded to turn the old barracks into the sumptuous pleasance we know. But even before any work was begun, he was already describing it to his brother Karl Ludwig as "the Schönbrunn of Mexico, built on a basalt crag, surrounded by Moctezuma's giant trees . . ." It was all in his mind's eye. One of Carlota's ladies-in-waiting found little to write home about except the drafts, leaking doorways and other inconveniences. Carlota prudently stuck to the beauties of the view. She wrote her father, Leopold I of Belgium, that it was "possibly one of the most beautiful views in the world, more so than Naples . . ." Taking full advantage of its lofty site, Maximilian and his European court architect built turrets and terraces like aeries. (He shared with his mad cousin Ludwig of Bavaria a taste for grandiose building.) To the despair of his treasurer he spent far more than he could afford on his "Mexican Schönbrunn" and increasingly irritated his French and English creditors, especially Napoleon III, who had committed his troops to the support of the Mexican Empire. The Mexican Imperialists, however, found the whole project most satisfactory. They fancied the idea of an imperial court, however improvised. The throne room was hung with chandeliers and gilded mirrors. Another room was lined with malachite. The state apartments contained all the bric-à-brac that any young Hapsburg couple would be expected to have: the silver was Christofle, the furniture, Boulle, the portraits, Winterhalter. To honor the famous view of the valley, as well as the memory of Miramar, their beloved seaside castle in Trieste, Maximilian named the new residence "Miravalle." The name never caught on, it didn't even last out the empire.

All Maximilian needed now was a short cut to his office in the National Palace. Remembering Baron Haussman's lucid remodeling of Paris, he opened a broad, straight causeway across swamps, country lanes and dingy alleys which ended in a monumental circus at the entrance to the city. Here stood Tolsà's equestrian statue of Charles IV, Mexico's cherished *caballito*, the "little horse" — that, after cantering all over town, stopped there for a breather in 1851 and did not move again for the next 130 years.

Landscaped along the lines of the Champs Elysées, the avenue was called *el Paseo del Emperador*, "the Emperor's Boulevard." It soon became the most fashionable residence in Mexico. Which leads us to a curiosity for anyone interested in money. According to the *Enciclopedia de Mexico*, land along the Paseo, which was worth one peso a square meter in 1865, had climbed to 20 pesos in 1893. Now (in 1981) you're lucky if you can find anything for 40,000 pesos a meter. However, for most of the 1865-1981 period, interest rates averaged 12%. At that rate you double your money every seven years, so one 1865 peso would double itself four times to 16 pesos by

1893. Meanwhile, the land had risen to 20 pesos per meter, which represented a real surplus value of 4 pesos. But if you continue doubling your money every seven years, you find that by its sixteenth doubling (in 1977) that single 1856 peso would have become 65,536 pesos, and now (in 1981) about 103,000 pesos, more than twice the value of the land the original 1865 peso could have bought. So much for speculators. Nothing beats compound interest.

The execution of Maximilian in 1867 completed the triumph of the Republicans. Carlota, who traveled through Europe vainly pleading her husband's cause, went theatrically mad during an audience with Pope Pius IX. She had to be confined in Miramar, then later in the castle of Bouchot, till her death in 1927.

The "Emperor's Boulevard" became the *Paseo de la Reforma*, in honor of Juárez's triumphant Reform Laws, and eventually the castle became the residence of the Mexican president. Porfirio Díaz, who occupied it longer than any other president, had married an aristocratic Creole lady and preserved the state apartments more or less as Maximilian and Carlota had left them, except, of course, for the throne room, which he turned into a bowling alley.

President Cárdenas, a militant populist, refused to be identified with such a place. When he assumed the Presidency in 1934 he moved into Los Pinos, a more modest mansion below the ramparts of the castle, where all succeeding presidents have also lived. This was a godsend to the people, for the castle has since been turned into Mexico's Museum of History and is open to the public.

The Zócalo

The traditional center of the city, towards which Maximilian had directed his Parisian boulevard from Chapultepec, covered roughly, during its first 400 years, the area of the Aztec Tenochtitlán and the Spanish city that Cortés built on its ruins. Its focal point is the *Zócalo*, an open square formed in Aztec times by the coming together of the four causeways that provided access to the shores of Lake Texcoco. This square, though its official name is *Plaza de la Constitución*, is popularly known as the Zócalo because of a pedestal, or socle, that was built there to receive a monument to Mexican Independence that was never completed. As a result, it has become the custom to refer to the central square of every Mexican town as "the Zócalo," whatever its local name may be, implying that, as in the capital, this is the square in front of the main church and the principal government offices. In the Zócalo of Mexico City the offices of the executive are in the National Palace, the enormously wide building of red volcanic rock that enclosed the entire east side of the square. It has been the seat of executive power ever since Moctezuma II built his palace there shortly after 1502 (which makes it the oldest consecutive seat of government in the hemisphere). Diagonally opposite to the National Palace, the Cathedral rather majestically closes off the northern end of the square. It stands adjacent to the spot where the Aztec's Great Teocalli ("House of the Gods") once stood. Why the Spaniards did not build their temple on top of the demolished pyramid is a mystery. Perhaps squeamishness — too much blood from human sacrifices? They did, however, use the ashlar stone blocks from its demolition in many of their early buildings. A massive serpent's head can still be seen in the cornerstone of the old colonial palace of Calimaya, now the City Museum, a few blocks south of the Zócalo.

The Tenochtitlán that Cortés and his men found in 1519 was a city very much like Venice in its early days. It was built out of a few islands formed by dredging the bottom of the lagoon. The tactical advantage was obvious: Lake Texcoco provided them with biggest moat in the world. Canals both divided and united the different *barrios* (quarters) and canoes provided the transportation. The north causeway led to the twin capital and principal market town of Tlatelolco, and thence to the hill of Tepeyac, the Aztec sanctuary of Tonantzin, now the sanctuary of the Virgin of Guadalupe. The south causeway went to Ixtapalapa and the flower and vegetable gardens of Xochimilco. The west causeway led to Tacuba, with a dogleg to Chapultepec for the aqueduct. The east causeway ran to a lakeside dock facing the town of Texcoco, on the most distant shore of the lake. According to contemporary accounts, Tenochtitlán was an extraordinarily beautiful city, with gardens bordering the canals, thriving commerce, crowded market places and magnificent palaces. Moctezuma had a botanical garden in his own palace as well as a zoo with freaks, dwarfs, hunchbacks and animals housed in an enormous establishment on the western edge of the city. The population was an estimated five hundred thousand and to the Spaniards approaching along the Ixtapalapa causeway from the south it must have seemed that the entire population had turned out to see their arrival. The rooftops were black with people and canoes crowded the waters on either side of the road. The horses filled the onlookers with awe. They thought the horsemen were precisely that: horse-men. (In Tlaxcala, during a banquet, the natives had offered the horses hot chocolate and turkey *tacos*.)

Moctezuma came out to meet the Spaniards with his retinue. His magnificence was vividly described by Bernal Díaz del Castillo, the soldier chronicler who set down his experiences many years later. Nothing escaped Díaz: the gem-encrusted gold soles of Moctezuma's sandals, the reverently downcast eyes of the noble lords who waited on him, the canopy of green feathers worked in gold and silver and fringed with pearls and turquoise. Cortés stepped forward to embrace the Emperor but was restrained by Moctezuma's attendant lords. So he simply presented the Emperor with a necklace of colored beads strung on a musk-scented golden cord.

Though Bernal does not report Moctezuma's words of greeting, they have been preserved for us in the Florentine Codex. He said, among other things,

> "Our Lord, you have wearied yourself, you have made yourself tired: now you have reached your own land. You have arrived at your own city. Here you have come to claim your throne. For a brief span, those who have already departed, your substitutes, have kept and guarded it . . . The kings who ruled and governed your city (have told us) that you would come again to install yourself in your seat and throne . . . and now it has come to pass: now you have arrived. Come to your land: come and repose: take possession of your royal abodes: give comfort to your body. Come to your land, O Lord."

Clearly, Moctezuma was convinced he was welcoming the Lord Quetzalcóatl in the person of Cortés. He led the Spaniard and his followers to his father Axayatl's palace on the western side of the square while he retired to his own on the opposite side, where the National Palace now stands.

This peaceful interlude did not last long. Eighteen months and many battles later, the Spaniards and their Indian allies – with a fleet of brigantines built in Tlaxcala and portered up piecemeal to Texcoco – laid seige to Tenochtitlán. The beleaguered Aztecs destroyed causeways, bridges, houses, everything that could be of any value to the besiegers. They buried their idols and dumped their sacred stones into wells. When Tenochtitlán fell, the Spaniards found a city of rubble and rotting corpses. The stench forced them to return to Coyoacán, the Tlaxcalans remained to feast that night on the limbs of their defeated enemies.

Cortés ordered the reconstruction of the Aztec capital along the lines of a Spanish city. His architect designed a grid more or less following the canals and centered on the intersection of the four causeways. The central city was reserved for

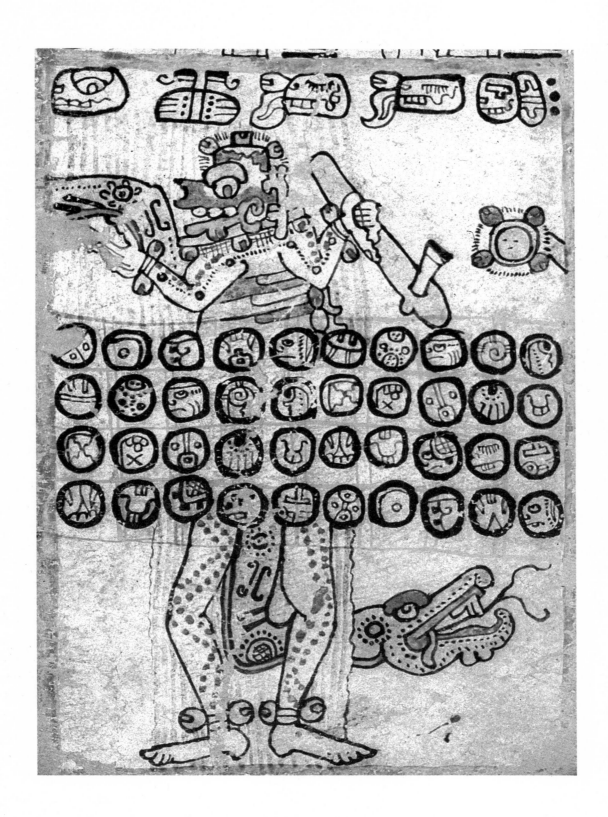

Spaniards, the Indians were sent literally beyond the pale. The canals were filled in and eventually the lake itself was drained to avoid the periodic and disastrous floods. Inevitably, the land filled in between the original islands was soggy. Just how soggy can be deduced from the swaybacked cornices and rooflines of many a colonial building: the prime example is relatively new, the Palace of Fine Arts which has sunk several feet below street level. (Modern engineering has solved the problem by using pilings or "floating" foundations.)

The National Palace

For political reasons, Cortés insisted on building the capital of New Spain directly on top of the Aztec capital. It would not do to move elsewhere and leave the natives free to return to the shrines of their ancient allegiances. The land itself was endowed with spiritual authority, so the true source and seat of power must remain where it had always been. For the same reason Cortés built his own palace on the site and foundation of Moctezuma's. Known as the "New Houses of Cortés" — to distinguish it from the "Old Houses" on the site of Axayatl's palace across the square — it was bought by the Spanish Crown from Cortés's son and heir, Martín, to be used as the official residence of the viceroys (one of whom was a descendant of Moctezuma, and another a descendant of Cortés).

It is curious to note that the viceroys held court seated on a velvet pillow under a portrait of the reigning monarch (an iconic custom now made universal by photography). This Moorish custom of sitting on cushions and carpets on state occasions survived in New Spain until 1700, when Philip V, the first Bourbon King of Spain, introduced some newfangled contraptions to the Spanish court: chairs.

In 1692, Indian rioters set fire to the Palace (there was no corn, no money, and a suspicion of hidden stores in the Palace itself). The damage to the building was soon repaired, but the surroundings remained squalid beyond belief. Contemporary records tell us about public latrines and vegetable stalls next to each other in the middle of the square. In 1789, almost a century after the Indian riot, a recently arrived viceroy, the second Count Revillagigedo, shocked by the filth he saw and smelled from his windows, set about cleaning up the mess. He cleared away the stalls and the itinerant merchants, ordered the level of the square to be lowered, then paved and fitted it with covered gutters for sewage and rainwater. During these excavations, the old Aztec calendar stone came to light, undoubtedly part of the sacred treasure the Aztecs had concealed during the last days of Tenochtitlán. By similar accidents, other important discoveries have been made. The building of the metropolitan subway, aside from casting up numerous idols and other objects, uncovered the small round temple in the Pino Suárez station, while a couple of electricians setting up a lamp post near the Cathedral hit solid rock instead of the mushy subsoil they expected and found another archeological stone that led to the Aztec *Templo Mayor*, now being excavated.

In 1793, during the same Viceroy's term of office, the square as we know it was taking shape, the south and west sides being much as they are now. In 1803, Tolsà's equestrian statue was unveiled on its handsome pedestal in a small oval garden at the south-east corner of the square. After having been moved, since then, to various sites in the city, the Caballito seems finally to have found a permanent resting place in a small plaza facing the Neo-Classical palace built by his own maker for the School of Mines. The horse, incidentally, was a percheron by the name of *Tambor*, "Drum." The illustrious Baron von Humboldt was present at the unveiling. Mexico City was at the peak of prosperity at the time. It was the golden age of the hacienda and the wealth of the second silver boom had not yet been dissipated. The hacendados and the mining millionaires, as well as the merchants and bankers who married into the aristocracy showed their wealth by building palaces and endowing convents, hospitals, schools and churches in the capital. Revillagigedo was a man of the Enlightenment, patron of arts and sciences, sponsor of expeditions, energetic enforcer of law and order. Alexander von Humboldt looked around him and was impressed. This was when he called Mexico "the City of Palaces," a description we cannot forget despite the mounting evidence to the contrary.

Like all wars, the struggle for Independence brought disorder, poverty, and destruction. No renaissance followed the peace; instead a series of revolutions and palace coups from which Mexico has never entirely recovered. In spite of the revolutionary blather, the country has so far only succeeded in finding stability and prosperity under the one-man rule of Porfirio Díaz, and under the one-party rule of the PRI.

Curiously enough, when independence was finally achieved, the spotlight of history turned away from the National Palace to blaze upon the nearby Palace of the Marquess de Jaral de Berrio, the owners of Tambor, incidentally, the percheron of Tolsà's equestrian masterpiece. An incomparable example of Mexican Baroque at its richest and most elegant, the palace had passed through marriage to the princely Sicilian house of Moncada. It was then occupied by a Conservative Creole officer, Agustín de Iturbide. Alarmed at the liberal turn that post-Napoleonic politics were taking in Spain, he decided to join forces with the Insurgent leaders to effect the definitive break with Spain in 1821. The Decree of Independence was ceremoniously signed in the palace which he occupied.

Iturbide showed his colors soon enough, promoting himself to Emperor and granting himself and his family huge possessions and impressive cash rewards. He insisted upon being addressed as "His Most Serene Highness" and adopted all the Napoleonic trappings of empire. Thus arrayed, he and his wife posed for countless portraits. A scant year later, he was tumbled from his pasteboard throne and sent into exile by the rebellious Antonio López de Santa Anna (of Alamo fame). Iturbide's empire did not last, though the palace from which he organized it, fortunately did. It has since been known as the Palacio de Iturbide and might again have become an imperial palace had Maximilian survived because Maximilian, having lost all hope that Carlota would give him a son, adopted one of the Iturbide grandchildren and named him heir to the throne.

When Iturbide's brief empire came to a close, the National Palace became once again the residence of the head of state. While preserving all its traditional functions, with the institution of the Republic, the palace now acquired many new ones. It had always housed the ceremonial apartments, the various ministries, the mint, the palace prison and the garrison, and now room was also found in its endless loggias, corridors and patios, to accomodate both the Senate and the Chamber of Deputies, as well as the Supreme Court. The separation of powers was clearly not taken literally in the early days.

Juárez was ousted from his quarters in the palace by the French Intervention, but returned after the defeat of Maximilian's empire. He died in office, in the bedroom he had always occupied in the palace. In Mexico, no armed takeover is ever considered successful if it does not culminate in the physical possession of the National Palace. The American troops realized that and flew the American flag from the central flagpole on the Mexican Day of Independence, two days after the Battle of Chapultepec. The 1910 Revolutionary factions fought over it as if it were the Republic itself. A cheery image from the early days of the Revolution has been preserved by the photographer Casasola's ubiquitous camera. After taking Mexico City, a group of revolutionaries took possession of the palace. They pose with their

51

rifles and sombreros behind Pancho Villa and Zapata. Pancho Villa is sitting on the gilded Presidential chair, bursting with glee, while the mustached Zapata on his left stares somberly into the camera's eye.

The palace is too old and has served too many masters to have come through history with its image untarnished. It is too big, and has always been too densely populated, teeming at all hours with equerries and maids and pages and soldiers and ladies-in-waiting and ushers and body-guards, and today with motorcyclists and secretaries and helicopter pilots and applicants for jobs and solicitors of official favors. One can imagine almost anything happening in the more florid periods of its past. Even Maximilian, a rather insipid paragon of a prince, turns out to have had a little side door for certain court ladies. His infidelities were no secret. In the country that invented *machismo*, even the Emperor had to prove that he could be unfaithful. The Palace now, however, under an uninterrupted series of PRI presidents, has become increasingly straitlaced and formal, in fact rather like what it was in don Porfirio's day.

The scattered remnants of our sumptuous past are many, but they tend to be overlooked amidst the far more numerous reminders of our stricken present. Skyscrapers rise where there is no room for a single additional car to park. Gardens mysteriously disappear. Communications are hideously clogged. Mexico City has been undergoing open-heart surgery since the early sixties when it was decided to revive its circulation by installing a metropolitan subway system (*el metro*) sufficient to its needs. The metro now moves millions of passengers a day, but is still only a by-pass. The population explosion is unabated: the heartbreaking truth seems to be that it is the poorest and the most deprived that multiply fastest of all.

Take the "Marías," for instance, those tiny Indian women who come down to the city from their native mountains rarely knowing more than a couple of words of Spanish. You find them always in the more affluent commercial neighborhoods, wherever there are people who can afford to be sensitive and charitable with their small change. They sit on the sidewalks of the *Zona Rosa* (the "pink-light" district, with everything that that implies), carrying their sucklers and surrounded by crawlers and toddlers in various states of undress. Many simply beg, though the more enterprising sell black avocados, peanuts or rape root (*jicama*), or else peddle packs of *real* American chewing gum and cigarettes (smuggled, of course, though one wonders who provides them with their stock in trade). They tread the same pathways toward Tenochtitlán and speak the same language as their Otomí forebears, and they are barely tolerated by the authorities, and exploited by them, exactly as they were in Moctezuma's days.

We are all Mexicans just the same. The problem now is simply that the melting pot is overloaded and cannot do its job.

23

22. *The Pyramid of Tenayuca. Chichimec culture, c. 1300 AD. Probably consecrated to the sun, this imposing edifice was built over, shell upon shell, no fewer than six times during the period before Tenayuca lost its importance in the early fourteenth century.*

24

23. *House of the Gilardi family, one of the most recent designs of Luis Barragán, the eminent Mexican architect.*

24. *House of the Gilardi family, interior. Dining room with pool.*

25

26

25. *Las Arboledas, a dividing wall. Another Barragán design.*

26. *The original Sanborn's, home of the department store and restaurant chain in Mexico City. The building is an eighteenth-century palace with an all-tile exterior showing the Moorish* poblano *style at its most elaborate.*

27. *Subway station at Pino Suárez, built around an original small Aztec temple.*

29

28. *Aerial view of the Paseo de la Reforma, laid out by the Emperor Maximilian to link his residence at Chapultepec with the center of the city. It was not finished until the beginning of the twentieth century. The veiled effect in this photograph is contributed by the smog of Mexico City.*

29. *General view of Mexico City. In the foreground, the Castle of Chapultepec, Emperor Maximilian's folly, which he fondly described as "the Schönbrunn of Mexico." Now Mexico's Museum of History, it is surrounded by the largest and most beautiful park in the city and still provides the best view of the valley from its many terraces.*

30. *Plaza de Santo Domingo, once the academic heart of the city. On the left, the church and cloister of Santo Domingo; on the right the Secretariat of Education; the corner building, now a department of the National Medical School, once housed the all-powerful Inquisition. The statue in the middle represents Josefa Ortiz de Domínguez, heroine of the Insurgency (1810-1821).*

31. *Capilla del Pocito. (The Church of the
Little Well), near the Basílica of Nuestra
Señora de Guadalupe.*

32. *Capilla del Pocito. Image of the Paraclete
in the first vault.*

33

34

33. *Garden patrol on a motor tricycle in the Alameda, Mexico City's central park.*

34. *Library of the National University. The new University City, of which the Library is architecturally the finest achievement, was built between 1950 and 1955 to house the National University of Mexico, founded in 1910 and granted academic freedom in 1919.*

35. *The Alameda. A Yucateca woman rests her feet by a fountain after watching the Independence Day parade.*

36. *Carrying the flag on 16 September, the Mexican Day of Independence. The Juárez monument is in the background.*

35

36

37

37. *The Gran Hotel de la Ciudad de Mexico. Art Nouveau glass in all its exuberance covers the main lobby.*

38. *The Cathedral. Gilded Baroque ornamentation, a metal balustrade and the fluted grey stone columns give an impression of the rich mixture of styles in this vast building, begun in 1573 and completed in 1813.*

39. *The gilded angel on top of the Column of Independence in the Paseo de la Reforma. This monument was inaugurated in 1910 to celebrate the first centennial of the Insurgency.*

38

40

40. The cloister of San Ildefonso, long-time
home of the Escuela Nacional Preparatoria.

41. Palacio Nacional, central courtyard.
The most cherished possession in the Palacio is
the bell which Hidalgo rang in Dolores. Each
year on 15 September at 11 p.m., the President
of the Republic appears on an outside balcony of
the Palacio to ring the bell and give the "Grito
de Dolores" to mark the beginning of the
ceremonies and the festivities commemorating the
Proclamation of Independence.

42. Ministry of Education. Mural, entitled
"Fraternity," by Diego Rivera, who painted a
total of 235 panels in this building alone.

41

42

44

45

43. *Lake of Xochimilco. Boats for hire in the floating gardens.*

44. *Lake of Xochimilco. Boatman with sweetcorn for sale to visitors in the floating gardens.*

45. *Father fiddling and son collecting money outside a subway station.*

46

46. *Cement architectural block surrounding the crater of an extinct volcano in the center of the city.*

47. *"El Caballito" (The Little Horse), Mexico's most famous statue and one of the largest equestrian statues in the world, stands at the junction of the Paseo de la Reforma and Avenida Juárez, where it was removed from the Zócalo in 1852. The sculptural masterpiece of Manuel Tolsà, it is a representation of Charles IV of Spain who died in 1803: an inscription explains that it has been preserved not out of affection for the Spanish monarchy but for its value as a work of art.*

48. *The Castle of Chapultepec. A turret on the upper terrace.*

47

48

50

51

49. Crowds gather in the Zócalo to shout "Viva Mexico" and "Viva la Independencia!" on the eve of 16 September, Mexican Independence Day.

50. The Cathedral, illuminated for the anniversary of Mexican Independence.

51. The Zócalo, the central square of Mexico City, with the facade of the Palacio Nacional on the far side. This building, which is the seat of the Mexican government, stands on the site of the new palace of Moctezuma II, or Xocoyotzin (The Younger). Rebuilt by Cortés in 1523, it became the residence of the Spanish viceroys from 1562, and was set on fire by rioters in 1692; rebuilt again, it was altered in 1820, and later by the Emperor Maximilian. A new floor was added in 1927.

49

Chapter 2
The Route of Cortés

The States of Yucatán, Campeche, Quintana Roo, Tabasco, Veracruz,
Tlaxcala, Puebla.

The Discovery of Mexico

The first recorded sighting of what is now Mexico occurred in 1517. Bernal Díaz del Castillo was the chronicler of the first expeditions and the *Conquest of New Spain*, as he called his book, is still the best guide on the subject. Three boats under the command of the rich hidalgo who financed the expedition reached the north-eastern coast of Yucatán twenty-one days after leaving Cuba. Sighting a large settlement with white stone temples, they were convinced that they had reached Cathay, the land of the Great Khan, so they named the city "the Great Cairo."

The first two expeditions failed to gain a foothold on the mainland. The second expedition, under Juan de Grijalva, brought back enough gold trinkets taken from the Indians of Tabasco to make Diego Velázquez, the governor of Cuba and financial backer of the expedition, a rich man. The glint of gold worked up enormous enthusiasm for further explorations. Velázquez set about organizing a third expedition. He put up part of the money, but as he had no intention of leading it personally, he looked about for a partner who would put up the rest and take charge of the entire venture. Many aspirants came forward. In the end, Velázquez settled on Cortés, against the advice of his courtiers.

Since dropping out of Salamanca, Cortés had led the picaresque existence typical of a poor hidalgo's son whose ambitions far exceeded his means. He shipped out to Cuba, eventually settling down in the eastern city of Santiago. In time he made a modest fortune farming, mining and acting as a free-lance lawyer on the side.

This was hardly the life he had dreamed of. In 1519 he was 34 years old, his time was running short. So when Velázquez chose him to head the third expedition, he mortgaged his lands and houses, sold his Indians, and invested the total proceeds in the eleven-boat expedition. Velázquez began to have misgivings. As the date of departure approached, Cortés was warned that Velázquez was replacing him, so he set forth before the appointed day and thereby foiled the governor's plans.

The official purpose of the expedition was to record events and map the western seas; to rescue the Christians from a previous sortie reputedly kept in captivity; to win the Indians over to the service of his Catholic Majesty, Charles V, to instruct them in the Christian faith, "and as a sign of submission to him to send great quantities of gold, gems, pearls and other things that they might have . . ."

Reaching the island of Cozumel, east of Yucatán, Cortés set about tracking down the shipwrecked Spaniards. Only two had survived. Of the two survivors, one had taken a native wife and had sired several children who thus became the first true Mestizos in the land. He had gone completely native and had no desire to leave his family. The second, Jerónimo de Aguilar, being a cleric, had remained celibate. When he presented himself before Cortés in a canoeful of Indians, Cortés asked, "Where is the Spaniard?" One of the naked, sunburnt men, with only a loincloth "to cover his shame" spoke up: "*Soy yo*," he said. Even his accent was strange. He unwrapped a small Book of Hours from a bundle of tattered clothes as proof of his identity. Cortés took him aboard, gave him "Christian" clothing, and from that moment on, Aguilar, with his knowledge of the Mayan language and customs, became an invaluable assistant.

The expedition then sailed along the coast of Yucatán toward the mainland until reaching the great Grijalva river of Tabasco, named after the Spanish captain who had discovered it. It was on that occasion that the natives had showed themselves so friendly and given Grijalva and his men the gold which had so excited Velázquez and the other Spaniards in Cuba. Now, however, they were definitely hostile and Cortés, landing, had to fight his first battle, in which he acquitted himself like a seasoned campaigner. The Indians were defeated by their own ceremonial approach to war as much as by the surprise of Spanish firearms and horses. They jumped and yelled instead of attacking, throwing fistfuls of dust and leaves up into the air to conceal their dead comrades from the enemy.

The Indians finally surrendered. Gifts changed hands — glass beads for gold again and twenty slave women "to cook" for the Spaniards on their boat. When asked where the gold came from, the Indians pointed west, repeating the words "Culhua" and "Mexico," which meant nothing even to Aguilar. The Spaniards left on Palm Sunday after mass. The slave women were baptized. Then, to the Indians' astonishment, one by one the iron warriors kissed a cross made of fresh cut saplings before they returned to the boat. Thus Cortés, his Mercedarian chaplain and his soldiers established the ritual they were to follow after every landing and every victory in the course of the Conquest of Mexico.

The Founding of Veracruz

The best gift Cortés was ever to receive was an inquisitive, restless, good-looking slave woman, who pestered Aguilar, asking for the names and uses of things. Her own name was Malinali, so they baptized her Marina, which was as close as they could get to it in Spanish. Her usefulness was not recognized until they reached the desolate sand dunes of what is now Veracruz. There Cortés, landing again, finally came face to face with Moctezuma's ambassadors. Nobody understood a word they said except for Marina. They spoke Náhuatl, her native tongue. She translated into Maya, and Aguilar then passed it on in Spanish. Her resourcefulness far exceeded her usefulness as a translator. After Veracruz, she became indispensable to Cortés, whose bed she came to share as well as his thoughts. She was wily, tactful, possessive. By her desire to please the Spaniard, she turned herself into a diplomatist of genius. She presented him to the natives in the best possible light, lacing his proposals with the euphemisms and compliments that still constitute the most effective passport for Mexican travel. After his eventual triumph, Cortés gave doña Marina a handsome settlement and married her off to one of his own men, Juan de Jaramillo, who is recorded as having got almost too drunk to attend his own wedding. Mexico remembers her with great cruelty as a betrayer of her people, conveniently forgetting that her own people had sold her into slavery. Her name has given us the word *malinchismo* to indicate the servile adoption of foreign values and customs in preference to our own, regardless of their merit. It is a term of profoundest scorn which does injustice to the memory of doña Marina.

In Veracruz, Moctezuma's ambassadors failed to persuade Cortés to take the Emperor's gifts and go away. In a last desperate attempt, Moctezuma sent Cortés those treasures which were soon to astonish Europe. It was, of course, exactly the wrong thing to do. Nothing could persuade the Spaniards to turn back after they had seen the gold and silver jewelry spread out on the sand and a helmet full of gold.

Realizing their mistake, the Aztec ambassadors disappeared as unexpectedly as they had come. The Spaniards faced a dilemma. To remain in the vast emptiness could mean either death by starvation or on the sacrificial altars of the obviously powerful Moctezuma. To return to Cuba meant sacrificing honor, glory and treasure to Velázquez, and probably being excluded from future expeditions. The stranded Spaniards were divided between those who were loyal to Velázquez and those who urged Cortés to conquer the land, though this was not the expedition's purpose.

Taking a legalistic line, Cortés found a way to bow to the will of the latter group, which coincided nicely with his own ambitions. He called on the expedition's scrivener to testify that on a certain day — and he chose Good Friday as being suitable — the Rich City of the True Cross (Veracruz) was founded in the name of their most Catholic Majesties. Aldermen were chosen, and as the new city lay outside Velázquez's jurisdiction, Cortés, whose authority derived from Velázquez, formally tendered his resignation. The City Council accepted it, considered the situation, and presently summoned Cortés to inform him that they had elected him Chief Justice and Captain General, agreeing also to give him a fifth of the expedition's proceeds after the deduction of the royal fifth. The whole thing went like clockwork.

A few days after the Aztecs had vanished, other Indians appeared who inadvertently showed Cortés the way to defeat Moctezuma. These Totonac Indians, sent by the Fat Cacique of nearby Cempoala, informed Cortés that the Aztecs were hated throughout the land. The Fat Cacique – so fat he could not come personally to greet the Spaniards – begged them to visit him in Cempoala. Cortés accepted and lived to bless the day. The Fat Cacique became his first and greatest ally.

The Burning of the Boats

After that events came thick and fast. Five arrogant ambassadors from Moctezuma arrived to scold the Fat Cacique for befriending Cortés, and demanded twenty sacrificial victims to erase the affront. Cortés prevailed on his host to take the Aztecs as prisoners and give them a sound thrashing. "The act was so astonishing," Bernal tells us, "that they said it must be the work of *teules*, which means gods or demons," a name which stuck to the Spaniards. The same night, Cortés himself freed two of the prisoners and sent them off to Moctezuma as living proof of his good faith.

The Cempoalans were terrified of the possible consequences of their actions. Cortés promised to defend them if they would swear fealty to Charles V, which they immediately did. The Fat Cacique then offered Cortés a fat princess, his own niece, as a bride, and seven other maidens for his men. Cortés accepted on one condition, that the Cempoalans abjure their idols, forbid the prostitution of boys dressed as women, and accept Christ as their Lord. (Another Totonac custom was to get drunk by means of *pulque* enemas, a filthy habit, though perhaps the least objectionable way of taking pulque.) The Fat Cacique and the priests agreed to see what could be done about sodomy, but on no account would they give up their gods. At this, Cortés and his men swarmed up the pyramids and demolished their idols while the Cempoalans cowered below in terror. When nothing happened – the sun went on shining, the earth did not swallow them up – the Cempoalans recovered their spirits and embraced the Spaniards affectionately.

News from Cuba reached Cortés in Cempoala. Velázquez was in a fury. He was trying to bring influence to bear on the Spanish court. Hearing this, Velázquez's friends plotted to desert Cortés and steal away on one of the ships. It was then, faced with the possibility of defection, that Cortés "burned his boats," in the traditional phrase, though in fact he only ran them aground and dismantled their rigging.

The Spaniards left Cempoala in August, 1519. They could move more easily now; the Fat Cacique had provided them with many bearers. They climbed up toward the central plateau by way of Jalapa. The intense cold was something they had not foreseen. In Xocatlán, a city loyal to the Aztecs, they found "more than one hundred thousand skulls" neatly piled in the temple square. The local Cacique tried to make Cortés turn back by describing the greatness and power of Moctezuma. But his descriptions of Moctezuma's treasure only made the Spaniards forget their cold and hunger in their eagerness to reach Tenochtitlán.

The Tlaxcalan Campaign

The independent seigniory of Tlaxcala, correctly described by the Cempoalans as the principal enemy of the Aztec Empire, proved to be every bit as hostile to the Spaniards. Having successfully resisted all Aztec attempts to conquer them, they had no intention of surrendering their independence to others. "There were so many warriors that they could have blinded us just with fistfuls of earth," said Bernal. They fought rather more cleverly than that, giving battle in such broken terrain that the Spaniards' horses were of little use. They killed a mare to show that the horses were not immortal. In short, they set about disproving the Spanish teules' supposed divinity. Several inconclusive battles took place before the Tlaxcalans sued for peace.

News of the Spanish victory over the hitherto undefeated Tlaxcalans flashed across the land. Five Aztec nobles immediately appeared in Cortés's camp. Aside from the usual gifts, they brought dire warnings of the Tlaxcalans' treachery, and the surprising news that Moctezuma was willing to submit to Charles V and send him yearly tribute providing that the Spaniards stayed away from Tenochtitlán.

The Tlaxcalan elders, for their part, begged him to visit their city. They provided 500 bearers for his cannon and calmed his suspicions by offering themselves and their families as hostages. Cortés finally accepted and Tlaxcala received the Spaniards with a joyful celebration. The Tlaxcalans offered their noblest maidens to the Spaniards. As in Cempoala, Cortés refused unless they agreed to abjure their idols and adopt Christianity. Being more spirited than the Cempoalans, the Tlaxcalans refused so energetically that the Mercedarian chaplain advised Cortés to let them be.

The most Cortés was able to achieve for the time being was the use of a newly whitewashed temple for the Virgin Mary and the christening of the Tlaxcalan princesses, who were given such peninsular names as doña Luisa and doña Elvira and then parceled out to his captains. Cortés destroyed the cages where men and women were being fattened for sacrifice, as he did afterwards in every town he entered.

A tug-of-war now ensued between Moctezuma's ambassadors and the Tlaxcalan elders. Each sought to win Cortés's trust. Moctezuma, fearing an alliance between Spaniards and Tlaxcalans, sought to effect a separation as soon as possible. He proffered a courtly invitation to Tenochtitlán and suggested that Cortés take the road through Cholula, where he and his men would be well looked after. The Tlaxcalans told him it was a trap. He should take the road through Huejotzingo, a town held by loyal friends and allies.

After much deliberation, Cortés chose the road through Cholula. The Tlaxcalans, though hurt by this sign of mistrust, offered an escort of ten thousand men, assuring him that he would need them. Cortés accepted only one thousand.

Cholula was a beautiful city of towers and temples. It was the sacred city of Anáhuac, and the Tlaxcalans refused to enter it. Cortés and his captains were lodged in a palace with a large courtyard, but shortly after their arrival they saw that they had indeed been tricked by Moctezuma. They were provided with firewood and water, but no food. Nor did the local chieftain appear to welcome them. More ambassadors arrived from Moctezuma, now insolently ordering Cortés to go no further. The Tlaxcalans sent word that 20,000 warriors were deployed in the countryside to slaughter the Spaniards. Doña Marina, talking to an old Cholulan woman, confirmed the rumor. The Cholulans had even sacrificed seven Indians to assure the success of their plans.

Cortés lost no time. He announced to the Cholulans that he was leaving early the next morning and would need 2,000 porters to accompany him to Tenochtitlán. The Cholulan nobles, priests and warriors were laughing, Bernal says, when they gathered in the forecourt of Cortés's palace the following morning. Their glee vanished when Cortés, interpreted by Aguilar and Marina, spoke to them from astride his horse. He itemized the details of their plot against him, mentioning even the pots of salt, chili peppers and tomatoes waiting for the flesh of the twenty live Spaniards who were to be sacrificed in a ceremony of thanksgiving. He upbraided them for their treacherous methods. The priests and caciques admitted the truth of these accusations, adding that they were merely obeying their lord Moctezuma. After hearing their confession, Cortés gave the signal. A shot was fired, and the slaughter began. Musket and cannon were emptied into the ranks of the Cholulans. The killing spread through the city, and temples and towers were set on fire. The carnage, fuelled by the Tlaxcalans' ancient enmity to the Cholulans, was so atrocious, that Cortés had to intercede in their favor. When a semblance of order was restored, Cortés pronounced his usual homily to the Indians, ordered the town to be whitewashed, and set up a cross as proof of the impotence of the Mexican idols before the power of the Christian God. After Cholula, there could be no further doubt about Moctezuma's intentions.

The fact that the Spaniards were obviously mortals and not teules had not entirely dispelled the idea that Cortés might still be Quetzalcóatl's avatar. After all, the Plumed Serpent in his time had also appeared in human guise. Now, as Cortés approached the valley of Anáhuac, a comet appeared and flared nightly above Tenochtitlán; while Popocatépetl spouted a vertical column of black smoke.

When the Spaniards crossed the pass between the volcanoes and descended toward the city on the lagoon, Moctezuma yielded to his fate. He donned his fine cotton cloak, his gem-studded sandals, his tiara of gold and, accompanied by the noblest lords of the realm, he walked to receive Cortés, begging him to enter and rest himself and take possession of his city.

The Neighboring Republic of Yucatán: the States of Yucatán, Campeche and Quintana Roo

Mexicans affectionately refer to the whole of the Yucatán peninsula as "The Neighboring Republic of Yucatán," though it now comprises the three separate states of Yucatán, Campeche and Quintana Roo (pronounced "raw"). To the traveler, until very recently, it suggested Mayan ruins and the charming "white city" of Mérida.

Roads are a recent development in Yucatán. In 1865, when the Empress Carlota decided to visit Uxmal, she had to ride all the way out from Mérida on a mule. Now a network of paved roads has made the archeological centers easily accessible, as well as the iridescent beaches of Quintana Roo. The traveler can drive from the posh seaside resort of Cancún to that most poetic of Mayan ruins, the seaside temple of Tulúm perched on a cliff above the many-colored Caribbean. If so inclined, he can continue southward to the Guatemalan border or cut west across the jungles to the walled city of Campeche on the Gulf side, and to the oil platforms of Ciudad del Carmen. He can bathe in magical lagoons along the way or watch the chewing gum trees grow, for this southern jungle of Yucatán is the source of most of the *chicle* chewed in the world today. The chico zapote (*Achras zapota*), or sapodilla tree, grows forty to fifty feet high, has glossy small leaves and the most delicious fruit imaginable. The chewing-gum is made from the rubbery latex drawn from its trunk. Chewing chicle has been a Mayan habit since prehistoric times.

How chewing gum got from Chichén to Chicago makes a curious story. When General Santa Anna was defeated in San Jacinto, he was held prisoner in Washington. The young officer detailed to keep a watch on him observed that he was constantly chewing something that he never swallowed. He asked what it was and Santa Anna offered him a piece from a small loaf he carried in his pocket. The officer found the chewing so pleasant that he decided to share the pleasure with the rest of the American people.

Campeche (from the Maya, *kam*, snake, and *pech*, tick – not an inviting place name) provided the door through which the Spaniards finally entered and conquered Yucatán. The east and north coasts of the peninsula proved impregnable. Montejo the

Younger, a son of one of Cortés's captains, was left with the task of colonizing the area after his father had given up in despair; he first fortified himself in Tabasco and, when he had achieved the necessary strength, launched his ultimately successful assault on the Mayan bastions of the peninsula.

From the beginning, a bitter rivalry existed between the fortified port of Campeche and the island city of Mérida. The *campechanos* resented the political domination of the northern city. Being the doorway to the peninsula, Campeche had to withstand the constant attacks of pirates during colonial times and, after Independence, even an attack from Santa Anna's navy in 1842. After much political maneuvering and a genocidal struggle between the Mayas and the rest of the population, Campeche finally achieved statehood in 1858.

Quintana Roo, on the eastern flank of the peninsula, did not become a state until 1974, though the federal government had separated it in 1902 from Yucatán, whose government had proved unable to cope with the sporadic and fierce rebellions in the area, where most of the unsubdued Mayas of the War of the Castes had taken refuge.

The modern state of Yucatán has thus been reduced to a triangular territory of calcareous rock, sinkholes and Mayan ruins in the north of the peninsula. It has consolations, though. Quintana Roo can boast of Cancún, Tulúm and Cozumel; Campeche, of its precious woods and offshore oil, but Yucatán has kept its character and its people, the ineffable *yucatecos*.

Physically and culturally they form a race apart. Though descended from the Maya, they did not inherit the elegantly tapered profiles preserved in classic Mayan art. The likeliest explanation of the difference is that classic art portrayed princes, priests and warriors of high breeding, whose heads were artificially shaped from birth to an ideal standard of beauty. Babies' heads were banded soon after birth to produce the characteristic elongation of the profile, while a bead of turquoise or jade was placed on one side of the bridge of the nose to tease the baby's eye inwards. However strange this description may sound, the results were stunningly beautiful, as may be seen in the carved heads of Palenque and Copán, or the clay statuettes of Jaina. This beauty did not, however, denote any great degree of amiability, which is the essential trait of the present day yucateco. When other regional stereotypes are discussed, their more notable defects are pointed out along with their virtues. Thus the diligent and devout *poblano* (from Puebla) is thought hypocritical; the cheery and entertaining *jarocho* (from Veracruz) can be coarse; the *regiomontano* (from Monterrey) an admirable citizen, and empire-builder, is stingier than a Scot; the *tapatío*, from Jalisco, is one hell of a guy, but carries the macho chip on his shoulder at all times; the *norteño*, from the northern border states is as open-handed as he is open-minded, but an inverted snob, proud to be a bronco. Only the yucateco has escaped invidious classification. His countrymen readily agree that he is bright, slightly nutty, and totally sympathetic.

But the phrase "The Neighboring Republic of Yucatán" is not a joke. It is a historical fact. Yucatán – the whole peninsula – did at one time secede from Mexico to form an independent state. The War of the Castes, in 1847, coincided with the Mexican-American War. The savagery of the Mayan rebels, who aimed at the extermination of all the Creoles and Mestizos in Yucatán, was unparalleled.

Yucatán, in 1839, had already seceded, and, now Mexico being at war, no help could be expected from that quarter. Desperate appeals were sent from Mérida and Campeche to Washington, London, even Spain, vainly offering the sovereignty of Yucatán to whichever government could provide immediate military aid. The rebels were at the same time getting arms and rum from the English in Belize, so it was not very realistic to solicit help from London. Only the coming of the rains put an end to this first and most violent onslaught of the War of the Castes. The rebels went back to plant their fields before taking up arms again. By that time, peace had been re-established between the United States and Mexico (1848), and the central government was able to send Yucatán help against the rebels. As a result of this, Yucatán finally and definitively joined the republic.

Yucatán's offer of its sovereignty to foreign powers is not as disloyal as it seems. It, after all, had little reason to consider itself part of Mexico. Yucatán was not conquered by Cortés but by the Spanish Crown. Its close political links with Mexico dated only from 1821. Given its history, Yucatán developed a strongly independent, therefore federalist, spirit. When Mexico became monolithically centralist between 1835 and 1846, Yucatán rebelled and, following the example of Texas, broke relations with the central government in 1839.

The War of the Castes lasted long after 1848, though it never again came so near to winning its objective. About two-thirds of the population of Yucatán perished in the initial years of the war. The surviving rebels retreated to the south-eastern jungles, where they continued to receive rum and bad advice from the British. They refused to sign a truce with the government of Yucatán, declaring they would govern themselves according to their ancient customs. They did, however, promise not to attack the Creoles. They had given Queen Victoria their word and they intended to keep it.

The Twine Binder and the Agave

The agricultural revolution that took place in the United States after the Civil War sparked a movement of intensive mechanization, which was to benefit a Yucatán drained of men and resources by the War of the Castes.

In 1875, George Appleby invented the twine binder for use with the machine harvested cereals. The demand for binder twine was enormous. Its supply was found in the *henequén* agave, which grew wild in Yucatán, thriving on its poor soil despite drought and neglect. After 1875, vast plantations of henequén were grown throughout the peninsula. (Since the twine was shipped out of the port of Sisal, this became the generic name for any agave fiber.)

The sisal boom and the great haciendas coincided with Porfirio Díaz's long and generally peaceful dictatorship. The sisal fortunes created an atmosphere of prosperity in the cities and of European luxury in the town houses of the hacendados. Things went swimmingly until 1900, when prosperity ended as suddenly as it had begun. The International Harvester Corporation formed a trust and quickly beat down the price of sisal by stopping all purchases. The planting of henequén lost all interest for the growers. In any case, the Revolution took the decision out of their hands in 1910. The Agrarian Reform parceled out the haciendas to the peasants who had neither the capital nor the time to cultivate the slow-growing agave. Seeking the advantages of a monopolistic control, President Cárdenas created the Gran Ejido Henequenero to control the national supply of sisal fiber, but the bureaucrats who managed it simply got rich while the ejidatario languished. World War II gave the moribund industry a brief boost, but the invention of synthetic fibers finally killed it. In 1955 the Gran Ejido was liquidated and the twine industry became a state monopoly.

So the state of Yucatán, which once lorded it over the entire province, is now the poor relation living on subsidies from the federal government. The islands and beaches of Quintana Roo have become international tourist attractions.

Torrents of chicle continue to bubble out of its southern jungles. Campeche has oil, shrimp fisheries and cattle. Yucatán, like an impoverished aristocrat, has kept its pedigree and its traditions, the underground lagoons and sacred grottoes, the richest ruins and the poorest lands. And, of course, the ineffable yucatecos.

Tabasco

Most of Tabasco is quite flat, and moreover excessively wet. Bounded and irrigated by the two largest river systems in the country, the Usumacinta and the Grijalva, Tabasco has been called the Mexican Mesopotamia.

Until roads were built is the 1950's, the villages and towns of that waterlogged state formed a kind of inland archipelago of isolated communities. The shaded groves of cacao, the chocolate bean, have continued to flourish as they did when Cortés and Bernal Díaz first wrote about them.

Tabasco had been growing fat like its cattle and its cattlemen since the Revolution. The oil boom of the late seventies put an end to its tranquillity. Oil poured money into the state, creating thousands of jobs, and outrageous prices for food and shelter. Even the landscape has changed, slashed by the pipelines, airstrips and new roads connecting the oil fields. Herds of plump, pale Brahma cattle, attended by the flocks of snowy egrets that perch on them for ticks, now graze near giant gas flares erupting from fields and lagoons. The sheer activity of the airport in Villahermosa, the state capital, is an indication of the change. Tabasco has now become once more a terminal, as it undoubtedly was in Olmec times, that is, a specific place to go, rather than to go through, which is what it became in the days of Cortés and the younger Montejo.

During the entire colonial period, Tabasco remained singularly becalmed. Lacking great wealth, it avoided trouble. In 1815, during the War of Independence, it repudiated "the ridiculous Mexican congress" and swore "blind obedience (to) our sovereign, señor don Fernando VII." In 1821, it calmly accepted independence. In 1846, at the beginning of the war with the United States, Commodore Perry — later of Japanese fame — steamed up the Grijalva to the state capital and demanded immediate surrender. Perry's gunboats opened fire and the Tabasqueños fired right back. After two days and several fruitless attempts to land, Perry retired: this was the one unequivocal victory over the United States.

Tabasco, then, has been rich and poor and is now rich again. To those who believe that the Word outlasts Wealth, however, Tabasco will never again be considered poor. It produced two of the greatest Mexican poets of this century, Carlos Pellicer and José Gorostiza. Pellicer was born in 1899, Gorostiza in 1901, both in Villahermosa. One a tropical imagist, dripping with color, the other an austere metaphysical poet. Together they represent the flesh and the mind of the Mexican sensibility.

Veracruz

Wedged between Yucatán and Veracruz, Tabasco had little chance to develop a distinctive image of its own. On the one side were the mythical, ruined cities of Yucatán, thronged with the ghosts of a fabulous past, to absorb the traveler's imagination; on the other, the vivid life of Veracruz to intoxicate him with the music of harps and guitars, with singing, lovemaking, and the promise of the immediate satisfaction of every appetite known to put the human soul in danger of mortal sin.

In Yucatán, the past outweighs the present. In Veracruz, the scholars think of the past and the politicians of the future, but to the jarocho-in-the-street, the present is all. So let us here choose a guide closer to our own time, deserting the incomparable Bernal Díaz del Castillo for a tireless, curious and wickedly observant Scotswoman who arrived in Veracruz in 1839.

Fanny Calderón de la Barca (née Frances Erskin Inglis) was the wife of Spain's first envoy to Mexico after Independence. She was possessed of a sharp tongue and a warm heart – and allowed ample scope to both in her journals and letters.

Few love affairs have begun as unpromisingly as Fanny's with our country. She hated Veracruz on sight. "Anything more melancholy, *délabré*, and forlorn than the whole appearance of things cannot be imagined. On one side the fort (San Juan de Ulua), with its black and red walls; on the other the miserable, black-looking city, with hordes of large black birds, called *zopilotes*, hovering over some dead carcass, or flying heavily along in search of carrion." The sand dunes described by Bernal grew in Fanny's eyes to "mountains of moving sand, formed by the violence of north winds." The cookery was "the worst of Spanish, Vera-crucified, but loads of it . . . garlic and oil enveloping meat, fish and fowl, with pimentos and plantains, with all kinds of curious nasty fruit which I cannot yet endure." She found the weather in December "*very* sultry," concluding that "this place which now seems like Purgatory must in summer, with the addition of the *vómito negro* (as they here call the yellow fever), be truly a chosen city!" Fanny's reactions may seem excessive but her descriptions were probably accurate. The unending civil wars and the plague had left Veracruz blackened and dilapidated. The one attractive house Fanny saw belonged to an English merchant. She could not understand the city's reputation as "a gay and delightful residence in former days, though even now those who have resided here for any length of time, even foreigners, almost invariably become attached to it; and as for those born here, they are the truest of patriots, holding up Veracruz as superior to all other parts of the world." Yes indeed: "*solo Veracruz es bello*," "Only Veracruz is beautiful," the jarochos still like to say.

Now, of course, Fanny's own name must head the list of those who succumbed to the enchantment of Veracruz. When she left the country two years later, she gave a glowing account of the building and heroic defense of San Juan de Ulua. And the food! "Veracruz cookery, which two years ago I thought detestable, now appears delicious to me! What excellent fish! – and what incomparable *frijoles!*"

All the same, her first impression was understandable. The seaside approach to Veracruz discourages the traveler. The landfall presented "a bleak and burning desert, which might well have deterred a feebler mind from going further in search of the paradise that existed behind." The jungle of Eden, which Douanier Rousseau marched through with Napoleon III's troops and years later painted from memory, is in the hinterland. Fanny saw it a few days after her arrival, the thick leaves with pink spikes, the hidden monkeys and lurking tigers, when she and her husband visited General Santa Anna at his lush hacienda, Manga de Clavo. But its "beauty and fertility" could not hide the unhealthiness of the place. One look at the Santa Anna family told her all. "He is yellow, his wife and daughter are green."

Even now, with its worst drawbacks eliminated by science and air conditioning, Veracruz is not a tourist resort. It is too uncompromising, a bustling international port with teeming docks, warehouses and markets, inhabited by a pungently idiosyncratic people. The casual vistor cannot work up any interest in its provincialism, the early evening *paseo* around the plaza, the open-air social club for lovers and strolling musicians, for vendors of ices, lottery tickets, pastries, baby parrots and adult macaws, for jumping children and clusters of gas-filled balloons. The domino-players, the beer and coffee drinkers, the café politicos, favor the marimba music of the arcaded *portales* around the square, while the floodlit City Hall transforms the plaza into a stage set.

Yet the traveler who remains long enough to get beyond the noise, the swearing, the jiggling of *La Bamba*, can be, in the end, quite enraptured by the town. Jarochos take a sly pleasure in observing the conversion of their visitors. They utter their classic phrase, "Only Veracruz is beautiful," and the new convert is likely to agree.

How It Happened

From the time of its wholly imaginary but perfectly legal founding by Cortés, Veracruz has been the foremost port of Mexico. For more than a century it remained Europe's only door to the New World.

Before long, Veracruz became Europe's door to the Orient as well. The Philippines — the real Indies Columbus had looked for but missed — had been clearly placed on European maps since Magellan discovered them in 1521. Contrary winds, however, had made trade impossible between them and New Spain until the discovery, in the 1560's, of the easy, though roundabout, return route — north to Japan, thence east to California, and down the coast to San Blas and Acapulco. The Manila Galleon brought silks, porcelain, ivory and spices, which the powerful merchant-shippers from Mexico City and Puebla sent on to Spain through Veracruz. Thus the establishment of the overland Veracruz-Acapulco link finally provided the long sought European route to the Orient.

In 1522, Cortés imported a lot of sugar cane from the Canary Islands and built an *ingenio* — a sugar mill — in the fertile hinterland of Veracruz. The industry prospered but the Indians collapsed. Negro slaves were brought in from the Caribbean islands. They survived in their new occupation and multiplied so rapidly that in 1602 they were strong enough to stage a rebellion and escape from their Spanish owners. In 1609, the Crown recognized the justice of their cause, granted them liberty and a tract of land where they founded the town of San Lorenzo de los Negros, now called Yanga after their original rebel leader.

The Pirate Problem

The silver strike of Zacatecas in 1548 made Veracruz the most tempting morsel for privateers in the New World. Millions in bullion were sometimes stored there, waiting to be picked up by the Spanish fleet. There were pirates of every nationality, but historical circumstances favored those who sought the protection of the English, Dutch or French sovereigns, Spain's traditional enemies. These were outraged at Pope Alexander VI's presumption in splitting the newly discovered lands of Africa, India and the New World between Spain and Portugal. It became a matter of honor to arm and license corsairs for the purpose of acquiring a share in the wealth of the New World. In New Spain, the cities of Campeche and Veracruz were the main targets. The depredations of John Hawkins and Francis Drake in the 1570's and of the Dutchman — Laurent de Graff — "Lorencillo" a century later, obliged Spain to build fortifications around these towns. The walls of Campeche are still standing, as are those of San Juan de Ulua, both equally useless.

The Hacienda

When Fanny and her husband visited General Santa Anna, she called his estate a *quinta*, or country house, though it comprised 900 square miles. She could not know, so soon after her arrival, that such estates were known as "haciendas" in Mexico, nor could she yet imagine the importance of the role the hacienda had played in the development of the country.

The principal precursor of the hacienda, the encomienda, appeared in the first years after the Conquest. In theory, the Spanish encomendero, or beneficiary of the encomienda, undertook all responsibility for the Indians in his charge, indoctrinating them in the Christian religion and protecting them from their enemies. His native encomendados, in turn, were obliged to work for him a certain number of days a week. Since the encomendero was usually a soldier avid for riches, not converts, the relationship easily degenerated and the encomendero himself became the worst enemy of the Indian he was supposed to protect.

The missionaries abominated the encomienda. They agitated violently in support of the Indians, even taking their cause to the Council of the Indies and the King himself. The Crown eventually paid heed and promulgated the New Laws of 1542, legally abolishing the encomienda. Despite the howl set up by the encomenderos, the Crown slowly but surely deprived them of all their *de facto* privileges. A royal decree of 1591 declared all land in New Spain to be Crown property. They could however, purchase the land from the Crown if they wished to obtain clear title. After 1615, all lands lacking proper title were auctioned off. By 1648, most properties had been legalized and the ex-encomendero or his descendants could take full possession of their lands. It was these properties that became the first haciendas.

Land, however, was practically worthless without the Indians' free labor, so the landowners devised a means of nailing down the native population. Playing on the Indians' innocence in money matters, the hacendado extended credit to his peons in the hacienda's commissary — the *tienda de raya* — far beyond the peon's ability to pay. Since he could not legally leave his employer while owing him money, this practice inevitably resulted in a system of serfdom through debt. Such debts were passed on from father to son. Eventually, the peon and his family became part of the hacienda's inventory and their debt was included in the purchase price of the hacienda. Though manifestly unjust, the system proved remarkably stable. The government of the New World colonies was an intermittent affair at best. Communications between Spain and New Spain lagged from two to four years behind events. Matters had to be decided on the spot by the strongest man around, who was frequently the hacendado. As lord of the manor, he had *de facto* jurisdiction over his peons.

The hacienda was taking its definitive form about 1630, when the first silver boom was petering out. The failure of the mines plunged the country into a severe depression. Bands of marauders preyed upon the countryside, driving the independent peasant to seek protection either in the nearest town or the nearest hacienda. Many sold their holdings to powerful hacendados and went to live within the hacienda walls. The hacienda thus became the unit of survival for the rural population during the seventeenth century. Every hacienda became self-sufficient, with bakeries, founderies, carpentry and leather shops, stables, dairies and sheep runs. In the pulque and cattle haciendas of the central plateau and the north it was said that the only things that they did not produce were salt, sugar and coffee. In Veracruz, with its giant haciendas extending from the coast to the mountains, the hacendados theoretically could produce everything, especially salt, sugar and coffee.

When money from the second silver bonanza began flowing again in the course of the eighteenth century, the hacienda reached the peak of its prosperity. Countless impressive *cascos* — hacienda compounds — appeared in the Mexican countryside, with churches ranging in style from the Plateresque simplicity of the Renaissance to the splendid ornamentation of the Churrigueresque Baroque and eventually Neo-Gothic.

The mainly agrarian character of the 1910 Revolution virtually brought about the end of the hacienda system, though miraculously a few haciendas have managed to survive from the sixteenth and seventeenth centuries to the present day. Others have gained a new lease on life as hotels and *paradors*, like the splendid casco of Galindo, near Querétaro. And still others are now true quintas — the country houses of the rich of today.

Jalapa (Náhuatl: *xalli*, sand, *apan*, river)

The famous hinterland cities of Veracruz developed like the hill stations of India as a refuge from the "black vomit" (yellow fever), cholera, malaria, and dysentery of the coast. The first sizeable settlement was Jalapa, which was already a thriving Indian community when Cortés marched through it in 1519, and is now the capital of the state. Like a giant urban staircase, it connects the tropical valleys of the lowlands to the bleak, cold plain of Perote. Halfway up, on a broad landing, is the administrative, cultural and commercial center of the city. There orchids grow on the trunks of the jacarandas near the stone balustrades of a small park, and there the mangoes, sapodillas, avocadoes and bananas from the valley below climb up the steep streets while the plum trees, pears and apples descend from the upper reaches of the town. The more prosperous Veracruz merchants and their families retired to Jalapa during the summer months. In colonial days, a trade fair was held in Jalapa after the arrival of the Spanish fleet from Cádiz in Veracruz; the fair achieved such prominence that the town came to be known as "Jalapa of the Fair."

Orizaba (Náhuatl: *Ahuilizapan, aahuiliztli*, joyful, *apan*, river. This difficult name was licked into shape by the Spanish tongue through gradual changes to Aulizaba, Ulizaba, Olizaba and finally to the very Castilian Orizaba.)

The snowy mantle of Mexico's highest (5,747 meters) and most symmetrical volcano (which last erupted in 1687), the Peak of Orizaba, is the first landfall of a sea voyager bound for Veracruz. Fanny Calderón de la Barca saw it a full week before arriving in Veracruz. The Aztec name for it is Citlaltépetl, "Star Mountain," and its gleam on the darkest nights served as a beacon for wayfarers.

Like the Fat Cacique's Cempoala, Orizaba was a Totonac tributary of the Aztecs at the time of the Conquest. When the Spanish troops got restive and demanded the bounty they had fought for, Cortés was forced to grant them encomiendas. He gave Orizaba to Jaramillo, doña Marina's husband-to-be, who, with another Spanish encomendero, practically exterminated the Indian population. Spanish settlers, attracted by the excellent soil and climate, soon repopulated the area. It quickly became a prosperous agricultural community. In 1873, the Mexico-Veracruz railroad passed through Orizaba, a recognition of its importance that also assured its future prosperity.

Breweries and textile mills were soon established in Orizaba's temperate plain. This industrial concentration, coupled with the tropical volatility of the Veracruzano temperament, produced one of the earliest tragedies of the Mexican labor movement. The workers of the huge textile plant of Río Blanco went on strike in 1907, to protest against the 14 hour work day and the banning of all newspapers and visitors in the laborers' quarters. Workers in neighboring mills followed suit. The militia was called out and the soldiers fired on the unarmed workers. Twenty-four hours later, 140 workers had been killed. Out of 7,000 workers, 5,000 returned to their posts. A few escaped, and the rest were sent in labor gangs to the "chicle inferno" jungle of Quintana Roo. Though the strike proved inconclusive, it is regarded, together with the Cananea Consolidated Copper Company strike of the previous year, as the starting point for the organized union movement which culminated in the enlightened labor legislation of the 1917 Constitution.

Córdoba

The rebellion of the negro slaves was indirectly responsible for the founding of this charming town. Yanga's rebels having become a menace to all traffic on the Mexico-Orizaba road, a fort was built for the protection of wayfarers and was manned by thirty volunteers from Huatusco. In 1617, those same men founded Córdoba, which has since been known also as the City of the Thirty Cavaliers.

Córdoba takes its aristocratic antecedents seriously and, fortunately, its rich farmlands have given it the means of living up to them. Yet in the end, it is the astonishingly varied beauty of Veracruz that seduces the traveler rather than the historical accomplishments of its inhabitants. The emblem of Fortín de las Flores —gardenias floating in a blue swimming pool — is a poor symbol compared to the spectacles provided by nature at every turn: the sheer drop from Acultzingo in the clouds to the intensely cultivated valley of Orizaba, the conical peak of Citlaltépetl reaching up to the stratosphere; the coffee plantations near Huatusco under a canopy of shade trees, the lagoon of Catemaco; the giant trees with the sapling, vines and epiphytes springing from the crotches on the highest branches.

One smiles at the jarocho's pride of place, but at certain moments the most jaded traveler may find himself saying, "*Solo Veracruz es bello ...*"

Tlaxcala (Náhuatl: *Tlaxcalli*, tortilla, a maize pancake)

This state is the smallest in Mexico, carved out of the giant Intendancy of Puebla in 1793 by the second Viceroy Gálvez, of Chapultepec fame. In contrast to Veracruz, man and not nature has created Tlaxcala's most impressive monuments.

For modern Tlaxcala it has all been downhill since the eighteenth century. Despite its valiant efforts to keep abreast of the times, nothing in its recent history can match its pre-Hispanic political and military development, nor the architectural splendor of its Colonial past. Fortunately a sufficient number of buildings are still standing to attest to the latter, while a history of the former was written for us a few decades after the Conquest by Diego Muñez Camargo, a Mestizo whose Tlaxcalan mother had lived through many of the events recorded by Bernal.

The earliest chroniclers called Tlaxcala a Republic for lack of a better term for this unprecedented federation of independent seigniories. Four states were involved, each represented by a lord or elder. Three of the lordships were hereditary, the fourth was elective. Though women were excluded from voting, they could inherit lands and possess goods independently of their husbands. A polygamous but tightly knit family life was the foundation of Tlaxcala's stability, and men who remained unmarried after the age of twenty-two suffered the indignity of having their hair cropped. Though trained in warfare since earliest youth, the Tlaxcalans were not unlettered Spartans. They several times defeated the bards of Texcoco and Tenochtitlán in their poetry contests. The four elders deliberated lengthily and publicly on problems affecting their common interests. Such a situation was singular enough in a time of absolute monarchies: what made it even more so was the fact that, whatever the decision reached and whatever its results, the elders forgot their objections and defended it unconditionally. Such disciplined unanimity enabled them to resist the armies of the Aztec empire with a minimal loss of life and land, and to accept their defeat by the Spaniards with a minimal loss of dignity.

Generations of ritual warfare — the "Wars of Flowers" for the taking of sacrificial victims — had developed a fierce hatred between Aztecs and Tlaxcalans. Though the wars had never caused significant damage to the small republic, the Aztecs had succeeded in severely limiting its trade. Tlaxcalans had no access to salt, sugar, cacao, gold or feathers, the last of which they seemed to have considered as essential as the first. They used wild honey for sweetening, and *tequexquite* (an alkali of sodium chloride and sodium carbonate) in place of salt. Feathers, gold and chocolate they did without.

When the Spaniards were put to flight from Tenochtitlán in the episode known as the Dismal Night — *La noche triste* — the Tlaxcalans proved to be foul weather friends as well as fair. They took in the mauled and defenseless Spaniards and literally nursed them back to health. On first seeing them, Bernal tells us, the elders wept.

The Tlaxcalans helped Cortés build the boats with which he proposed to beseige the great city on the lake. The elder Xicoxténcatl – don Lorenzo de Vargas since his baptism – gave Cortés the ten thousand warriors he requested, and offered as many more as he might need to carry the boats to the shores of Lake Texcoco.

After the Conquest, the Tlaxcalans followed Cortés on his voyages north and south and were instrumental in the colonization of New Spain and Central America. Pedro de Alvarado took his Tlaxcalan bride with him on the conquest of Guatemala, where she bore him the first Guatemalan Mestiza, doña Leonor de Alvarado.

The grateful Cortés granted them special privileges, later confirmed by the Crown. These included keeping their exclusively Indian government, exemption from all tributes, the right to bear a coat of arms, to ride horseback, to be addressed as dons, and to work for their own benefit whatever mines they found, as well as the lands they already possessed and those that were later granted to them.

Cortés founded the city of Tlaxcala in 1520 on an uninhabited plain, in order not to impinge on the autonomy of the new city as a senatorial council. When the Franciscans arrived in 1524, they agreed to divide their efforts in four missions: Churubusco, near Mexico City; Texcoco; Tlaxcala; and Huejotzingo. The establishment of the Franciscan convent in Tlaxcala began the building spree – no other word suggests the exuberance of the results – that turned Tlaxcala into a veritable treasure house of ecclesiastical architecture. The friars imposed their Plateresque version of the Renaissance on the earliest buildings. The walls, the corner chapels and the facade of the Convent of San Francisco, for example, reflect this classical austerity. As they began to work on the interiors, the Indian craftsmen, having mastered the technique of iron tools, began to get out of hand. Their work grew elaborate in the gilded retables (reredos) behind the altars, the turned grilles and the airy Moorish style of the beamed and coffered ceilings. By the middle of the eighteenth century, both friars and native craftsmen got completely carried away. The Sanctuary of Ocotlán, on a hilltop outside the city, is an enchanting summary of their joyful art. Towers of spun sugar rest on bases faced by orange-pink tiles. The white shell facade juggles lightly with all the elements of the Baroque, and the traveler enters the church begging for more. The interior, rich as it is, comes as a disappointment after the breathtaking originality of the facade. Many turn back at that point, not knowing that the plum is hidden behind the main altar, the Virgin's Chamber, a tall octagonal well rising through carved gold to a jubilant vision of glory above. A single Indian craftsman by the name of Francisco Miguel carved it in the 1740's, possibly thinking that his scrolls, volutes, columns and polychrome divines represented a realistic inventory of Heaven's furnishings. Whether accurate or just plain giddy, his vision continues to dazzle and astonish.

"Woe is Mexico!" goes the saying. "So far from God, so close to the United States." Tlaxcala must have felt the same about the Spanish Crown and its local representatives. A few decades after the Conquest, faithless officials began to disregard the privileges and exemptions granted them by Cortés and confirmed by the Crown. In 1583 a delegation of Tlaxcalan natives, accompanied by the historian Muñoz Camargo as interpreter, traveled to Spain to demand the restoration of their privileges. Their mission may have succeeded because forty-two years later, curious about Tlaxcala, "whose inhabitants joined with Cortés and we may say were the chief instruments of that great and unparalleled conquest," the Englishman Thomas Gage visited the town and wrote of it:

"Tlaxcala is worth all the rest of the towns and villages between San Juan
de Ulua and Mexico . . . Its inhabitants were chief instruments for the
subduing of Mexico, and therefore to this day are freed from tribute by the

kings of Spain, paying not the money which as a tribute tax is laid upon
every Indian to be paid yearly, but only in acknowledgement of subjection
they pay yearly one corn of maize, which is their Indian wheat."

Tlaxcala has now fallen prey to all the tributes laid on it by a tattered economy in
a harried century, which makes its beauty doubly precious in that poor land.

Puebla   "Si a morar en Indias fueres,
         que sea donde los volcanos vieres."

"If you go to live in the Indies, let it be where you can see the volcanoes." Did
this piece of doggerel influence the choice of site for the city of Puebla de los
Angelos? It is anyhow sound advice. Notice the plural "volcanoes," which refer
unmistakably to Popocatépetl and Iztaccíhuatl. The two volcanoes can only be seen
simultaneously from the temperate valleys of Puebla, Morelos and Mexico City itself,
where the climate is more conducive to a long life.

In pre-Hispanic days, though fertile and well irrigated, the site was uninhabited.
Like Veracruz, Puebla was a city created by fiat. Unlike Veracruz, however, it was not
the result of a political coup but of detailed planning. Sensing the social threat posed
by the large floating population, the Second Audiencia decided to found a city for
these displaced Spaniards. Puebla was officially established in 1531 and paced out
according to the traditional design of a Spanish city: a central square, presided over by
the church and set in the middle of a grid of wide streets and square blocks. As an
urban experiment it served the double purpose of settling the surplus population and
protecting the route between Mexico City and Veracruz.

It flourished prodigiously. A few years later, the enthusiastic Franciscan
Motolinía called it the second most beautiful city in New Spain. Though it first
prospered as an agricultural community, industrial works and commerce soon
changed the character of the town. *Obrajos* (textile mills), the first glass works of
Mexico, and shops displaying ceramics in the Talavera style so loved by Spaniards,
replaced the stables and orchards that had originally filled the city blocks. Presently
the textile mills moved out to the country. In their place, nunneries, monasteries, and
churches appeared, and the locally produced tiles and bricks covered the facades of
the larger houses producing the colorful, even gaudy effect of the *poblano* style (the
outstanding example is the House of Tiles — the original Sanborn's — in Mexico City).

Puebla's importance as a commercial crossroads, industrial center and
agricultural producer, made it a coveted prize in every national and international
struggle. The French suffered their greatest defeat there on 5 May 1862, in their first
attempt to take the city. Though General Zaragoza was the Mexican commanding
officer, the credit for the victory was given to the young General Porfirio Díaz and
won him a national following. And it was also in Puebla, on 20 November 1910, that
Aquiles Serdàn, his sister Carmen and his brother Máximo, fired the first shots of the
revolution that put an end to Díaz's thirty-year dictatorship.

The number of its religious establishments earned Puebla the reputation of being
a dour and "Levitical" city. That is certainly the impression it made on Fanny
Calderón de la Barca, who called Puebla "the Philadelphia of the republic," clean,
well-paved and dull. "Its extreme cleanness after Mexico is remarkable ... The ladies
smoke more, or at least more openly, than in Mexico; but they have so few
amusements they deserve more indulgence. There are eleven convents of nuns in the
city, and taking the veil is as common as getting married."

But then her hosts in Puebla (her hostess, too, reminded her of a Philadelphian,
"always with the exception of her diamonds and pearls" which she wore for breakfast)
never showed her any of the churches that might have made the alert and intelligent

Fanny revise her impressions. The Capilla del Rosario, for example, a Dominican chapel a few blocks from the Cathedral, would surely have delighted her. It belongs to the delirious and opulent Churrigueresque that developed so exuberantly in eighteenth-century Mexico. The Tree of Jesse branches out from the sculpted walls in boughs and tendrils of carved and gilded wood. It induces a kind of architectural vertigo, a sense of elation that one learns to recognize as the first symptom of Baroque addiction. It is certainly felt in the Virgin's Chamber at Ocotlán and, near the city of Puebla, in the San Francisco Acatepec and in Santa María Tonantzintla, that coloring-book paradise of the Indian's childlike faith.

Strangely, Fanny saw none of this. She notes that the houses are large and well built, "the Cathedral magnificent, and the plaza spacious and handsome," adding, on a later visit, "– and withal a dullness which makes one feel as if the houses were rows of convents and all the people, except beggars and a few business men, shut up in the performance of a vow." And this within a few steps of the riotous goings-on in the Rosary Chapel!

Cholula (Náhuatl: *cholollan*, place of highwaymen)

Mexican school children and readers of Hachette's *Guide Bleu* are still told that Cholula has 365 churches — one for every day of the year and each built on the site of a pre-Hispanic temple. Few visitors who actually go there try to count. Those who do quit after the first ten or twenty; too much dusty walking is involved. So the myth persists though after the holocaust and demolition of the *teocallis* by Cortés and his Tlaxcalans, only thirty-four churches finally went up, including the church built on the top of the giant pyramid which the Spaniards, despite all their efforts, were unable to destroy. This grafted-on Christianity never quite took, as though the fanaticism of both sides had rendered the soil sterile to further religious endeavors. Most of the churches are deserted and Cholula is now merely a bubbly-domed architectural curiosity, the ghost of a once sacred city. Where Christianity was not so violently imposed, however, it found a soil as fertile as any in the New World. One of these places is Huejetzingo, the friendly town the Tlaxcalans recommended instead of the treacherous Cholula. One of the four original Franciscan convents was founded there to take advantage of the large Indian population as a source of both labor and converts.

The monastery they began in 1528 is an impressively castellated structure. The gothic grace of its main portal reinforces rather than weakens the fortresslike front raised to face a hostile environment. The churches built in later centuries preferred to forget the stern realities of earlier times. In place of crenellations and high, unscalable walls decorative blandishments appeared verging on the flirtatious. In Santa María Tonantzintla and San Francisco Acatepec, two of the more splendid examples, the builders brought together tiles, niches, swirling columns and decorated dadoes that could serve as an anthology of the poblano style. Tonantzintla has become famous among students of the *teonanacatl* ("god's flesh" mushroom) cults of the southern mountains.

In Acatepec we find something else. The luster of gold and titles speaks less of the Indian's adaptability than of his aspirations. Raised in poverty and squalor, the laborers sweated to create the only palace they could ever hope to enter; to criticize the Church for its ostentatious magnificence is to miss the point completely. To the unlettered worshiper, visual and tactile beauty evoke heavenly bliss more vividly than the austere contemplation of the abstract Good. Order and richness supply the qualities most lacking in his daily life. To those who have nothing, opulence is all.

53

52. Uxmal (Yucatán). Detail of the Pirámide del Adivino (the Pyramid of the Soothsayer) c. 600-900 AD, a vast structure in the Maya tradition characterized by its distinctive oval plan.

53. Chichén Itzá (Yucatán). Temple of the Warriors and Group of the Thousand Columns, Maya-Toltec culture (after 950 AD). The colonnade extending to the right of the temple is an extension of the portico that once stood in front of it; both originally supported some form of roofing. Compare with the Toltec Pyramid of the Atlantes in Tula.

54. Chichén Itzá (Yucatán). A Chac-mool temple figure. These figures, which originated in the Toltec period, were named "Chac-mools" by the imaginative French archeologist, Le Plongeon. We still do not know their exact significance.

54

55. *Chichén Itzá (Yucatán). The Pyramid of Kukulkán, also known as El Castillo (The Castle). Kukulkán means "Plumed Serpent" in Maya, and the name derives from the two columns in the form of the serpents at the entrance to the temple on top of the pyramid, typical of Toltec architecture.*

55

57

56. *Chichén Itzá (Yucatán). The Observatory, also called El Caracol (The Snail) because of its spiral staircase, with El Castillo in the background.*

57. *Uxmal (Yucatán). The Palace of the Governor. A classic example of the Puuc "latticework" surface decoration.*

58. *Uxmal (Yucatán). General view of the ruins, with the Quadrangle of the Nuns in the background, the elliptical Pyramid of the Soothsayer on the right, and the ball court in the foreground. Courts of the ritual ball game are found in several of the archeological sites of this period (c. 600-900 AD).*

59. *Labná, near Uxmal (Yucatán). The Arch of Labná. This is a rare example of an architectural form not often found in Mesoamerican cultures; the Puuc style appears again in the decoration above the side doors.*

58

59

60

61

62

63

60. *Izamal (Yucatán). Loggia of the Santuario de la Virgen de Izamal, the church of the huge Franciscan monastery built in 1553-1561.*

61. *Chichén Itzá (Yucatán). The Wall of Skulls* (Tzompantli) *on top of which the skulls of sacrificed prisoners were displayed on poles. This detail shows human skulls carved in bas-relief at the base of the wall.*

62. *Tulúm (Quintana Roo). Temple of the Frescoes. Detail of wall-painting, Classic Maya period.*

63. *Tulúm (Quintana Roo). El Castillo (The Castle), the most impressive edifice in this ruined Maya city, seen across the bay. When Juan de Grijalva sighted Tulúm from the sea in 1518, he likened it to Seville; it was abandoned in 1544, when the Spaniards conquered north-east Yucatán.*

64

64. *Market scene in Yucatán. A banana seller surrounded by his wares.*

65. *Market scene in Yucatán. A woman in the street carrying a* papaya.

66. *Progreso, near Mérida (Yucatán). Wall-painting of La Virgen de Guadalupe in the market. This Virgin is the patroness of Mexico and her image has a place of honor in houses and villages throughout the country. The green, white and red electric light bulbs above are symbolic of the Mexican flag.*

67. *A road near Valladolid (Yucatán). Three children in front of their home at the end of the day.*

68. *Escarcega (Campeche). 5:30 a.m. – a child wears a jute rice-bag against the cold.*

69. *Tlacotalpan (Veracruz). Three children in front of a house in a flooded street. Floods from the nearby river Papaloapan are very frequent in this area.*

70. *Near the oilfields of Villahermosa (Tabasco). Aerial view of vehicle tracks crossing and recrossing the bare earth, showing clearly the surface impregnated by crude oil.*

67

68

69

71

72

73

71. *Oil flares near the Bermúdez refinery (Tabasco). Most of Tabasco is flat and very wet, in fact, 60% of its surface is water, only 40% land. The oil boom of the seventies has poured money into the state at a prodigious rate.*

72. *A flooded house in the state of Veracruz. In its early years Veracruz was scarcely more than a port of call where ships from Spain could find good harbor. They did not stay long because of the unhealthy climate of the coast. Even today, as a bustling city and port, Veracruz is known for its humidity, excessive rainfall and bad climate.*

74

75

73. Vast expanses of empty sand on the coast near Champoton (Campeche). This part of the coastline is hardly visited by tourists, and is used mainly for fishing and the cultivation of coconuts.

74. On the coast near Uzilam de Bravo (Yucatán). An abandoned wooden jetty.

75. Sabancuy (Campeche). A river on the coastline; the curious coloring is a purely natural effect.

76. *Young Indian Quetzal dancer with characteristic feather head-dress.*

77. *Cuetzalan (Puebla). Fiesta de San Francisco. Indians at prayer in the main church of this small picturesque Nahua town.*

78. *Cuetzalan (Puebla). Indians in the traditional costume dancing in front of the church at the Fiesta de San Francisco.*

80

79. *Ocotlán (Tlaxcala). The eighteenth-century sanctuary, one of the most original monuments of the Spanish Baroque.*

80. *Santa María Tonantzintla (Puebla). The main altar, richly decorated with polychrome carving by local artists in the Mexican Churrigueresque style (eighteenth century).*

81. *Cholula (Puebla). Private house on the way to Tonantzintla. This magnificent house displays the massive walls and crenellations that turned houses into fortresses for the protection of their inhabitants against marauding bandits.*

83

82. *Acatepec (Puebla). Saint and child in niche, in the church of San Francisco. The* poblano *style here clearly shows its Moorish origins. The flags are put here for the Fiesta de San Francisco.*

83. *Acatepec (Puebla). Church of San Francisco. Base of the entrance doorway, with gravestones.*

The Isthmus of Tehuantepec (Náhuatl: "the hill of the wild animal," from *tecuan*, wild animal, and *tepec*, hill).

The Isthmus is considerably more than the narrowest part of the Mexican mainland. This strip of land represents the geographical divide between North and Central America. Its barriers of jungles, swamps, rivers and mountains prevented any extensive mixing between the northern civilizations of Mesoamerica and the Maya of the south. After the Conquest, the centralist government of New Spain found itself cut off by the Isthmus from the dependencies of Yucatán, Guatemala and Panama, which developed their own centers of government. Thus the Isthmus effectively isolated the area to the east and south of it from the mainstream of Mexico's development.

A foreign traveler may find many things about this region puzzling. Our geographical references, for example, might strike him as quite irresponsible. We conventionally refer to the trans-Isthmian states as "the south-east," which is precise and proper for Chiapas and Oaxaca but hardly accurate for the Yucatán peninsula. The cornucopian shape of our territory is responsible for such cavalier usage. From a 1,800 kilometer northern frontier, Mexico tapers down at an angle of 45 degrees towards the 215 kilometer wasp waist of the Isthmus, which is definitely in the south-eastern part of the country. The fact that the broad shelf of Yucatán turns upward like the prow of a ship into the Caribbean seems to be neither here nor there. If it starts in the south-east, it just has to keep on being part of it. Another oddity resulting from the shape of the country is that we have no true south-west. A country cut on the bias is bound to lose huge chunks of reality. If we look for the south-west on a map of Mexico, we can see only the Pacific. Or almost. Barely visible, an archipelago of flyspecks, the Revillagigedo Islands can be descried on the same latitude as Veracruz and a straight drop down from Tucson and Guaymas. That, if anything, is our geographical south-west. The islands are rocky and uninhabited. Snakes and iguanas proliferate among the cactus. Small wonder no one mentions the south-west.

Chiapas (Náhuatl: *chia-apan*, river of *chia*, the *Salvia hispanica*, L. Capital: Tuxtla Gutiérrez, Tuxtla, from *tochtli*, "rabbit")

In pre-Hispanic times Chiapas formed an integral part of the Mayan civilization. Most local Indians are descended from the Maya, as are their languages and dialects. Chol, Tzeltal, Tzotzil, Tojolabal, Zoque, Lacandón are a few of them. The highland Indians, preponderantly Tzotzil and Tzeltal, are usually lumped together as Chamulas, though technically only the first should be so called. They have maintained their vigorous individuality through the centuries.

Their typical costume consists of a black woolen blanket with a headhole over a white smock (if single) or white britches (if married). It would look monkish except for the fringe of multicolored ribbons hanging from the rims of their flat straw hats. Their hilltop cemetery of San Juan Chamula is a place of poetry. A mound of earth marks each grave. An ordinary wooden cross stands at its head and a plank rests on the mound. But at the high far end of the graveyard rises a Golgotha of gigantic wooden crosses, twenty to thirty feet high, painted in all colors — green, brown, purple, pink — bearing witness before the vivid sky.

An Elegy for the Lacandones

"The Men of the Forest," Jacques Soustelle calls them in his excellent study, *The Four Suns*. They live in the rain and cloud forests between Mexico and Guatemala, a habitat Soustelle accurately describes as "this ocean of vegetation choked with water."

He visited six Lacandón *caribales* (hut clusters) and that accounted for nearly half of the total population of "perhaps two hundred Indians scattered over an area of nearly 39,000 square miles . . ." Soustelle's book recounts a trip he took to Lacandón country in the thirties. The 1976 *Enciclopedia de Mexico* estimates that no more than one hundred and fifty are left, though their numbers may have increased slightly in recent years.

"No structure can persist when society itself falls below a certain density," writes Soustelle. An agricultural people, the only technique they know is slash-and-burn, which forces them to periodic moves. They are totally self-supporting, growing their own food, and making their garments out of fibers they grow or pick wild. But planting their maize where mahogany, cedar and sapodilla once stood, and burning precious woods to heat their *tortillas* or roast an occasional monkey or parrot, means that they are literally eating their forests up.

The Lacandones are the only Indians in Chiapas who speak anything like the classic Maya. Authorities agree that they originated in Yucatán, and are the descendants of those peasants who, a thousand years ago or more, left the great cities of the Maya to rot and collapse under their own weight. Soustelle discards the theory of soil exhaustion as the principal cause of the Mayan decline. He places the blame squarely on the shoulders of the priestly mathematicians, who kept raising the taxes in order to finance the construction of ever more magnificent ceremonial centers, and to subsidize research into the nature and use of the zero and the positional value of numbers. These were achievements the peasants neither understood nor cared about. They cared about keeping for themselves the fruits of their own labor, and little by little, the peasant forebears of the Lacandones deserted the sacred towns and cities of the Maya. In the course of a few generations, the priests found themselves officiating in empty temples, with no one to draw water, hew wood, plant maize or carve stone. The forms remained, but the meaning had fled. The men whose work sustained this admirable civilization wanted simpler gods, the kind found among trees, caves and undefiled waters. Their kind seeped away into the forest where they took up the life of solitude and bare survival they still lead.

Palenque (Maya-Chol: "stockade")

Soustelle describes this process with particular reference to Palenque. That city of grey and golden monuments died when it was "deprived of its labor force and food supply; it became a brain without a body and died of starvation. The élite caste itself was dispersed, the avenues disappeared under the advancing brush and the first sprouts of the future jungle appeared on the steps of the pyramids and the roofs of the palaces."

Palenque had been dead six hundred years when Cortés and his men marched unseeing past it on their ill-starred expedition to Las Hibueras in the south. Centuries would elapse before modern archeologists began a systematic study of the site. Sylvanus Morley, the dean of Mayan studies, considered Palenque the most beautiful ceremonial center in the Mayan world. It is difficult to disagree. The superbly delicate architecture set in a jungle raucous with monkeys and birds in brilliant flight is irresistible.

Conquest and Colony

"We resolved that when we came to Tapanatepec we would choose our way according as the winds did favour or threaten us. However to Chiapa we would go . . . because we would see that famous and much talked of province of Chiapa."

So wrote Thomas Gage, a young Dominican missionary, in 1626. The winds he feared did in fact strand him and his companions on a narrow mountain shelf for three days, where they subsisted on water and the small sour lemons which they found growing nearby. Several times, when the winds rose in violence, he made his peace with God. When finally the wind subsided and his group reached the top of the mountain, "we perceived truly the danger so much talked of, and wished ourselves again with our green lemons in the way of Tapanatepec."

They had reached a fearsome ledge between the mountains and the sea.

> "The passage that lieth open to the sea may be no more than a quarter of a mile, but the height and narrowness of it stupefieth, for if we look on the one side, there is the wide and spacious South Sea lying so deep and low under it that it dazzleth the eyes to behold it; for if we look on the other side, there are rocks of at least six or seven miles depth, sight of which doth make the stoutest and hardest heart to quake and quiver. Here the sea expects to swallow; there the rocks threaten to tear with a downfall, and in the midst of these dangers in some places the passage is not above an ell [45"] broad. We needed better cordials for that quarter of a mile than feeding three days upon green lemons and water, and durst not man ourselves so much as to go through it upon our mules. We lighted, and gave the Indians our mules to lead, and we followed them one by one, not daring to walk upright for fear of head giddiness and looking on neither side, but bowing our bodies, we crept upon our hands and feet as near unto the tracks which beasts and travellers had made as we could without hindering our going."

Diego de Mazariegos, arriving in 1526, was the first European to gain a foothold and establish Spain's dominion over the land. His decisive battle with the Chiapa Indians took place on a bluff high above the Sumidero canyon, a deep gulley cut through the rock by the Grijalva river near Tuxtla. The gorge is as dauntingly sheer as the one described by Gage, but rather than surrender to the Spaniards, the desperate and defeated Chiapas threw themselves into the abyss. The Spaniard, shocked, ordered his men to cease fire and made every effort to reassure the terrified survivors.

Mazariegos located a cool and pleasant valley above Chiapa de los Indios and there, in 1528, founded a town which he named Villarreal. The First Audiencia changed the name "in perpetuity" to Villaviciosa, a singularly short-lived perpetuity since three years later it was generally known as San Cristóbal de los Llanos. This name became official with the city's Royal Charter in 1535, and lasted until 1829, when it was renamed San Cristóbal de Las Casas, in honor of its first Bishop, Bartolomé de Las Casas.

This militant Dominican is one of the most controversial figures in the history of New Spain. His lifelong mission was the protection of the Indians from the depredations of the Spaniards. He was as fearless in pursuing his mission as he was ruthless. His knowledge of his subject, however, was decidedly spotty. After Salamanca he had moved to the New World, where he acquired an encomienda on the island of Hispaniola. Revolted by the heartless exploitation of the natives, he returned to Spain, in 1514, the year in which the Laws of Burgos, the Crown's earliest attempt to legislate in favor of the Indians, were enacted. He therefore witnessed only the first and worst period of Spanish colonization, but that became his immutable point of reference. He spent the rest of his life agitating and engaging in polemics while he traveled back and forth between the Old World and the New. Storming over the paper and sealing-wax hurdles of the Council of Indies, he gained the ear of Charles V and succeeded in pushing through the New Laws of 1542, which formally abolished the encomienda.

123

Moral fervor being what it is, Fray Bartolomé soon had more enemies than friends. In Chiapas he was the first — and most hated — bishop. San Cristóbal was, after all, a town founded by and for encomenderos, and he left his see in fear of his life before a year was over. He returned to Spain to his writing and his disputations, and though he did not resign from his bishopric until 1550, he never came back.

His *Brief Relation of the Destruction of the Indies* made him a celebrity both in Europe and the New World. Rather than straight history, it is a denunciation of Spanish iniquity. Finally, even the seraphic Franciscan, Fray Toribio Motolinía lost patience with him and his incessant muckraking, and in 1555 wrote a famous letter to Charles V telling him so.

Muckraking however has its uses — reforms sometimes follow. Las Casas got the New Laws enacted, yet he gave the Spanish Crown scant credit for its concern with the Indians' welfare. He disregarded the fact that the Mendicant Orders had championed the Indian against the encomendero from the beginning. He gave his country and his Church the worst possible image. Consequently, though regarded by most official historians as the protector of the Indians, the more independent of them look on him as the originator of the Black Legend.

The political development of Chiapas predictably resembles that of Yucatán, and for the same reason: its remoteness from Mexico's center of power. The citizens of both provinces considered themselves Yucatecos or Chiapanecos first, and Mexicans only by contigency. Like Yucatán, Chiapas declared its independence from Mexico for a couple of years (1823-24). Its periodic Indian rebellions culminated, as in Yucatán, in a widespread genocidal War of Castes in 1868. Yet what reads like straight history in Yucatán can turn into slapstick in Chiapas, or degenerate into something unearthly and lurid.

Thomas Gage tells us about a "chocolate war" between the bishop and his flock that took place during his stay in San Cristóbal in 1626 or 27. It all began because the ladies of San Cristóbal loved their chocolate and could not go without it even for the length of a Mass. "It was much used by them," writes Gage, "to make their maids bring them to church in the middle of Mass or sermon a cup of chocolate, which could not be done to all, or most of them, without great confusion and interrupting both Mass and sermon." The bishop cautioned them, the ladies ignored him. The following Sunday they found nailed to the Cathedral door a threat of excommunication. The ladies were indignant and appealed to the Dominican Prior to intercede for them. He did so, but the bishop "answered that he preferred the honor of God and of his house before his own life." Some ladies defied his ban and continued "drinking in iniquity in the church, as the fish doth water. This caused one day such an uproar in the Cathedral that many swords were drawn against the priests and the prebends, who attempted to take away from the maids the cups of chocolate which they brought unto their mistresses." After that, "the city" forsook the Cathedral for the convent churches, where nuns and friars were more amenable to reason. The bishop countered by ordering the entire population to hear Mass *only* in the Cathedral, under pain of excommunication. The women preferred to immure themselves in their houses rather than yield to the bishop. "In that time the bishop fell dangerously sick and desired to retire himself to the cloister of the Dominicans, for the great confidence he had (in them). Physicians were sent for far and near, who all with joint opinion agreed that the bishop was poisoned, and he himself doubted not of it at his death . . . He lay not above a week in the cloister, and as soon as he was dead, all his body, his head and face, did so swell that the least touch upon any part of him caused the skin to break and cast out white matter, which had corrupted and overflown all his body." A prominent gentlewoman "was commonly censured. She was said to have prescribed such a cup of chocolate (to poison) him who so rigorously had forbidden chocolate to be drunk in the church . . . It became afterwards a proverb in that country, 'Beware of the chocolate of Chiapas,' which made me so cautious that I would not drink afterwards of it in any house where I had not very great satisfaction of the whole family."

The bitter rivalry between San Cristóbal and Tuxtla in Chiapas, runs parallel to that between Campeche and Mérida in Yucatán. The outcome, in Yucatán, was the creation of the separate state of Campeche. In Chiapas, on the other hand, the state remained whole, but the capital was moved from San Cristóbal to Tuxtla in 1892. The Spanish town's civic pride was the chief casualty. As late as 1911 the Bishop of San Cristóbal was still urging the natives and the neighboring Chamulas to attack Tuxtla and recover their honor.

The Chiapas War of the Castes took place in a world of the imagination where real blood was shed. A Chamula shepherdess one day found some "colored pebbles," which, she told her mother, "descended from heaven." The mother showed them to the headman of the village, who put them in a box and told everyone the following day that they had kept him awake all night long. They spoke to him, he said, they cried and beseeched him to take them out of the box. Such awesome news attracted a large public and the man founded a religious sect, declaring the shepherdess and another woman saints and burning incense before them. They bitterly felt the lack of their own Messiah, since, as they complained, the white man's Christ did not protect the Chamulas. So on Good Friday, 1868, before a gathering of several thousand Chamulas, the village chief, assisted by two female saints, crucified the shepherdess's younger brother, a child by the name of Domingo Gómez Chebcheb. While some of the faithful drank the blood from his limbs and from the cross, the rest danced and sang in ecstasy. Government authorities viewed the affair in a more somber light. They considered it murder; the Chamulas countered that it was a religious service. Unimpressed, the authorities arrested the celebrants and the war began. Thirteen thousand Chamulas attacked the barrios of San Cristóbal. After many skirmishes and countless deaths on both sides, the Chamulas were finally defeated and their leaders shot in the central square. From there the soldiery fanned out through the countryside, hounding the Chamulas out of their hiding-places and slaughtering them in their own villages.

Such episodes leave the reader stunned with horror. Still, some questions remain. How did that shepherdess think up the bit about the colored pebbles descending from heaven? And what led the Chamula chief to say they spoke to him and gave him instructions?

Historians dismiss these questions as pure local color witchery, yet anyone who has read R. Gordon Wasson's seminal studies on "entheogenic" ("God-within-us") mushrooms in Mesoamerica must immediately recognize the colored pebbles as the magic mushrooms of mycolatry. Wasson found in the Bibliothèque Nationale in Paris a post-Conquest Codex in which two men are shown speaking, their speech illustrated by blank, comma-shaped balloon-glyphs issuing from their mouths. Below them, lined up in a row, are four mushroom caps with a glyph issuing from each one of them. The two men are apparently involved in a trial and, according to the inscription on the Codex, are waiting to hear the mushrooms' opinion. The link between this tableau, the talking pebbles and the crucifixion of the Chamula boy seems clear.

The mushroom cult went underground with the advent of the Christian vine and wine culture, though in practice, as Wasson has shown, it continues to this day. There is ample documentary evidence to the effect that mushrooms and alcohol do not mix, either culturally or psychologically. The bestial excesses reported by the

Christian chroniclers as being produced by eating mushrooms seem rather to be the result of eating mushrooms when drunk or of drinking while eating mushrooms.

Oaxaca (Náhuatl: *Huaxyacac*, "where the gourds begin to grow," from *huaxi*, gourd, and *yacatl*, nose or tip, the beginning or end of something. Capital: Oaxaca)

"Mexico is a western country by day and an Indian country at night." So said José Vasconcelos, a writer and politician of extravagant gifts who once dreamed of cleaning up the Revolution. His statement is perhaps truer of Oaxaca, his native state, than of Mexico in general. Spanning all history, growing in dark places and observed respectfully only at night, the cult of the god-bearing mushroom weaves its thread through the life of the Oaxaceños.

Drugs and Sacrifice

After his year of earthly pleasure and adoration, the godly youth ascends the pyramid to his sacrifice, breaking his flutes and dropping them on the steps. A maiden and her attendants dance towards the temple of the Maize God. As she steps across the threshold, the officiating priest decapitates her with a single stroke of his gold-handled flint knife. The surrogate of the Flayed God is gorgeously bedecked before being flayed alive by the priest who will then don his skin. The priests who sacrifice to Huitzilopochtli drink the victim's blood from his still beating heart. The elegant serenity of the sacrificial victims is the dominant key of all the accounts of human sacrifice that have reached us. More than sang-froid, it amounts to a collaboration which mere respect for the ceremonial cannot sufficiently explain. In the ceremonial ball game, the captains of both teams were sacrificed, the loser for his unworthiness, the winner for his excellence. Yet knowing that death was the prize, both played as if to save their lives – or their honor.

The most likely explanation for all this lies in the drug culture of the pre-Hispanic Indian civilizations. Respect for ritual honor alone seems superhuman under the circumstances. Only the special influence of a drug would seem to give that kind of sustaining power.

Wasson's description of a "shamanic mushroom agapé" in Oaxaca, which appeared in LIFE, 13 May, 1957, spotlighted the whole subject. After the publication of his article, Oaxaca became the drug-culture Mecca of the western world. The Oaxaca present day shaman María Sabina blames Wasson for the vulgarization of the mushroom cult, yet Wasson's study is thoughtful, original and above all respectful. He could hardly be blamed for the vast crowds that descended on Oaxaca. The treasure of Monte Albán, Mitla, the achievement of the Dominicans are largely ignored. Beauty, art and courage cannot, alas, compete with the drama of drugs.

There are other simpler, yet more unexpected, sights that foreign visitors have to be dragged to see. The many-petalled stone laundry in the Convent of Santa Catalina, now an impressively vaulted and massive walled hotel. And what we call the tule tree a few miles outside the city. The dwarfish church beside it, is nothing you would cross the street for. Yet you look inside and find that it is of a quite respectable size. Then it dawns on you: how big *is* that tree? The answer is: enormous. Something the size of a small forest, growing from a single vast trunk that fifty men together can barely touch hands around. A two thousand-year-old cypress, that is perhaps the oldest living thing on the planet.

Before Cortés: Monte Albán

In the 1930's the archeologist Alfonso Caso explored a burial mound in Monte Albán, now known as Tomb 7, and there found a treasure of gold and silver jewelry, quartz vessels, jade and turquoise mosaics. The rich find captured the world's imagination. Suddenly everyone wanted to know more about Monte Albán, about the Zapotecs who built it, and about the Mixtecs who made the exquisite jewelry. Oaxaca experienced the first of its tourist booms in this century.

As with practically everything in Mesoamerica, Monte Albán began with the Olmecs. Two thousand years before Cortés, some Olmec groups left their steamy jungles on the Gulf coast and came to settle in the central valley of Oaxaca, a brisk 1,500 meters above sea level. They left massive foundations on Monte Albán, on which the Zapotecs later built their temples. The Monte Albán civilization, together with Teotihuacán and the classic Maya, dominated the entire classical period. All three were theocracies, ruled by a caste of astronomer-priests. Teotihuacán was the most influential, trading far and near throughout Mesoamerica and beyond it. The Maya were the most advanced mathematicians. Monte Albán's eminence, however, was and is literally physical: the astronomer-priests leveled a mountain top in the middle of the high Oaxaca valley in order to build their ceremonial center closer to the stars. The Mixtec name for Monte Albán, *Sahandevui*, means "at the foot of heaven."

The rectangular plaza is precisely oriented on the four points of the compass. The proportions of its surrounding structures, the alternating rhythms of staircases and entablatures, satisfy the most demanding criteria of classical harmony and equilibrium. A cosmic silence fills these heights. The astronomer-priests make their ghostly presence felt whenever they keep their appointments with the stars. In the last moon before the spring equinox, for example, a visitor standing on the southern platform looking north receives a clear sign from them at the end of the day. As the sun sets on his left, a full moon rises above the rim of the valley to the right. For an instant, the heavenly bodies hang in a perfect balance of celestial mechanics, until the seesaw tilts to the west and the sun disappears in a horizon of liquid gold, leaving Monte Albán to receive the full silver flood of the moon.

The withering away of the classic civilizations toward the end of the first millenium left a power vacuum which produced a period of warring states. The theocracies of the Classic period were supplanted by the militaristic societies of the Post-Classic. The Toltec-Chichimecs in central Mexico, and later in Yucatán, filled the spaces left by the Teotihuacaños and the Classic Maya. In the Oaxaca valley, the Mixtecs, longtime neighbors and allies of the Cholula Toltecs, emerged as the dominant people. They subjected most of the Zapotec cities. Though some intermarriage took place between the princely families, they arrived definitely as conquerors, driving the more recalcitrant lordlings out of the valley toward the coast of Tehuantepec.

Both Zapotecs and Mixtecs call themseleves "the Cloud People," which suggests a common origin in the cloud forest of Oaxaca's northern mountains. The Zapotecs were evidently the first to migrate to the valley. During the prime of Monte Albán, the Mixtecs were still slashing and burning down their primeval cloud forests. The gradual erosion of their land finally forced them down to the valley as well. By the time they got to Monte Albán, it was already an abandoned graveyard, and as such they continued to use it, borrowing their predecessors' splendor for their own dead.

Mitla

The Mixtecs settled in the Oaxaca valley about the year 1280, shortly before the Mexicas first arrived in Chapultepec. Mitla survived the Christian holocaust because it was *not* a ceremonial center but a complex of courts and palaces built by the Mixtecs in the vicinity of some Zapotec temples. From a distance it looks like a squat convent with some very ordinary cupolas and a sawed-off bell tower. Drawing closer, its Post-Classic character becomes aggressively evident: the corners of the building jut out, like a section of a pyramid placed upside down. The domes, it turns out, belong to a primitive Christian church behind the compound. The proportions of the low, long facades recall some of the secular buildings of the Classic Maya in Yucatán. The decorative detail, however, is unimaginably complex, like a sampler embroidered by an obsessively cubistic nun. Mitla is a jigsaw puzzle – the ultimate jigsaw puzzle. Thousands of little stone bricks are tightly and precisely fitted into geometrical patterns running like lightning along the horizontal friezes. It is the apotheosis of zigzag.

The Aztec Invasion

Between 1440 and 1470 the Aztecs, from the warlike north, finally ventured into the unyielding south. They were not at first strong enough to gain control of the Oaxaca valley, but sufficiently so to open lucrative trade routes to the cacao-rich lowlands of Tabasco and Chiapas. The cacao bean, after all, continued to be the accepted currency throughout Mesoamerica. A grandson of Moctezuma II, Fernando Alvarado Tezozomoc, wrote an account of one Aztec experience in Oaxaca in his *Crónica Mexicana* of 1598. On this occasion the inhabitants of Huaxyácac captured and slaughtered a caravan of Aztec merchants and robbed them of their merchandise. Moctezuma I sent a punitive expedition to raze the town and some years later, in 1486, Ahuízotl built a fort there in its place. This was the beginning of what became in effect the Aztec occupation of Oaxaca. The tax collectors followed close upon the warriors. The chronicler records a lengthy tax roll of which one example will suffice. The tribute of the single province of Tlaxiaco consisted of 400 large cotton mantles, a warrior's quilted armor and shield, 20 gourds full of gold dust, 5 bags of cochineal and 400 bouquets of quetzal feathers every eighty days. In 1507 a rebellion broke out against these outrageous taxes, and it took the combined Aztec forces of the Triple Alliance six years to suppress it. When Cortés's first emissaries arrived in 1520, they found among the Oaxaca Indians many ready allies against the Aztecs. The Zapotecs even sent troops to Cortés during the seige of Tenochtitlán.

The Marquess of the Valley of Oaxaca

Oaxaca is the phoenix of the Mesoamerican cities, rising from its ashes after every holocaust. First razed by Moctezuma I in 1468, it was replaced by an Aztec fort that was again burned to the ground by the Spaniards in 1521. Some Spanish officers engaged in a coastal campaign against the Mixtecs found the site so attractive that they abandoned their garrison and founded a town where the fort had been. Cortés, infuriated, ordered the town to be dismantled and evacuated and the founders to be brought back in chains. He wanted the valley of Oaxaca for himself.

The reason was gold. He was evidently acquainted with the Aztec tax rolls and coveted the wealth of the province. Cochineal, cacao, and quetzal feathers probably seemed small change to him; they only began to interest him after the carmine dye and the chocolate drink became the rage of Europe. Cortés distributed encomiendas in the valley among his illegitimate children and his closest friends. But a royal order arrived in 1526 ordering the site of Oaxaca to be divided into building lots. Cortés intercepted the order and routed the presumptive settlers for the third time. The following year he personally took possession of the valley and planted the first fields of wheat. During his absence in Spain in 1528, Charles V's city charter was made effective, and a Spanish city was founded with the name of Antequera. In the same year the first Dominican missionaries arrived. Thus, when Charles granted Cortés the title of Marquess of the Valley of Oaxaca in 1529 and named him Captain General of New Spain, Cortés returned in triumph but found that the city of Oaxaca-Antequera had been placed forever beyond his reach.

The Spanish Crown granted many encomiendas and titles to the conquistadors of the New World, but only four seigniories: the Duchy of Veragua to the descendants of Columbus; the Marquisate of the Valley of Oaxaca to Cortés; another Marquisate, in Peru, to a descendant of the Incas; and, in 1706, the Duchy of Atlixco (the jewel of the Plateresque near Puebla) to the Count of Moctezuma and Tula, a descendant of Moctezuma II who had been the thirty-second Viceroy of New Spain.

Cortés's title specifically included "the lands and vassals, the woods and pastures, all waters, both running and standing, and complete civil and criminal jurisdiction – all the rights in short, which belonged to the Crown itself in the aforesaid lands." Both Spaniards and Indians were included among his vassals, though only the latter owed him tribute. Cortés's grant, then, despite the exclusion of Oaxaca-Antequera, was the most magnificent of fiefs. It consisted of 22 towns, 23,000 vassals and 11,550 square kilometers of territory. The estate was not a single entity but lay scattered very selectively on some of the lushest land, the richest mines and the most populous regions of New Spain (next to gold, Indian labor was the most coveted form of wealth). It included Tacubaya, Coyoacán, Cuernavaca, most of the state of Morelos, Toluca, Tepoztlán, Mitla and eleven other towns in the Valley of Oaxaca. Tehuantepec also belonged to the Marquesado. The seigniory disappeared in 1811, blown away by the first rough winds of the nascent republic.

Dominicans and Indians: Convents and Communities

The Dominican Order was the first of the Mendicant Orders to establish itself in Oaxaca. It was instrumental in achieving for the first time a degree of political unity in the province, first by mediating between Spaniards and natives, and then by intervening among the Indians themselves, isolated as they were by their mutually incomprehensible dialects and their multitude of villages, each fiercely individualistic and jealous of its rights. Their early involvement in this basic problem made the Dominicans for a long time the dominant religious order in Oaxaca.

Most of the natives quickly accepted Christianity; only the priestly élite fought back. The Dominicans adopted as many of the local customs, beliefs and rituals as they could in order to make conversion easier for the Indians. The old gods were turned into Christian saints. Cocijo, the Zapotec rain god, was translated into Saint Peter, who manages rainfall for Christians. A Zapotec heroine, Pinopiaa, was worshiped at the same shrine as Saint Catherine of Siena.

The converted masses broke the Dominicans' missionary hearts by getting gloriously drunk at every festival. The Indians' weakness for alcohol undoubtedly accounts for the harsh pre-Hispanic laws against drunkenness. Only the threat of capital punishment could keep them on the wagon. A census of 1726 shows that in the Oaxaca Valley, 513 drinking establishments existed in 46 towns. The very first Christian wedding of natives after the Conquest ended in a drunken brawl. The groom, son of a great lord, was killed. Three days later his funeral took place "with all the pomp and solemnity that had attended the wedding celebration."

The Indians worked very hard, though, for their spiritual guardians. The Dominicans, not having taken a vow of poverty like the Franciscans, undertook commercial ventures and were able to build rich cloisters for themselves and even richer churches for God. The Convent of Santo Domingo in Oaxaca is probably the finest example of Dominican architecture in Mexico. Building was begun "with a few pennies" in 1547. The cloister, which now houses the Mixtec treasures of Monte

Albán, was finished in the following century. In 1659 the monks brought in a stucco artist from Puebla to decorate the vaults and walls of the church. He designed a tree and a bower and a vine whose tendrils of green and gold entwine the heads of cherubs and saints and Dominican precursors and missionaries, and present a synopsis of the Dominican order told in exuberant rococo against a dazzling background. The eighteenth-century Rosary Chapel opens up inside the church like an explosion in a gold mine. Yet, rich as it is, it cannot match the gaiety of the church itself. Purists will tell you that this is a sham, a very recent reconstruction. During the anti-clerical wars of the Reform (1858-61) the altars were stripped, the walls defaced and riddled by target practice. The church was used as a stable. True. But the fact remains that, sham or not, depending on your views about restoration, the interior of the church is a joy to behold.

A hundred and fifty years after the Conquest, the Dominican chronicler Francisco Burgoa tells us that "the Mixtecs still hold the lands and towns they conquered as principal evidence of their deeds. Even within the capital at Theozapotlán, in which I am writing, they had a stronghold, and they still occupy it as a barrio of this town, not to mention other places that they founded around it." But the same chronicler adds a sadly familiar tale about the hereditary ruling class. "The caciques nowadays are half as intelligent and twice as wicked as their predecessors. All the old caciques have died, and with them have gone their esteemed reputation and courage, as well as the cattle estates they once possessed. Their heirs, more absent-minded than vigilant, find themselves poverty-stricken. Their habits are corrupt; and when they lack outsiders with whom to quarrel, they stir up disputes and misunderstandings within the town . . ." Land has always been the bone of contention. The pre-Hispanic villages had their communal lands. After the Conquest, the Crown respected these comunidades based on their "primitive patrimony," and created further communal grants for the benefit of landless pueblos. The Indian thus became rooted to his soil and his immediate community. Though Spanish soon emerged as the lingua franca of the region owing to the multitude of dialects, the Indian languages continued to be spoken with undiminished vigor. They have reinforced the ancient community loyalties, leaving little or no room for broader ethnic or national sympathies. This probably accounts for the absurd political fragmentation of Oaxaca. With a population of 2.5 million, it is divided into 570 municipalities.

The encomienda – with the exception of Cortés's – never prospered in Oaxaca, and no vast haciendas developed here. The Indians had sufficient good land of their own, so that the hacendado could not lure them into debt peonage. Moreover, the Crown and the Church, mindful of their respective fifth and tithe, backed them solidly against the encroachments of Spanish and Indian landowners.

Twin Stars: Juárez and Díaz

It is perfectly true to say that in Mexico the nineteenth century started in 1810 with Hidalgo's *Grito de Dolores*, the first popular call for Independence, and ended in 1910, with the first shots of the Revolution.

Spain's eventual withdrawal from Mexico in 1821 left a power vacuum as obvious as that which followed the collapse of the Classic civilizations a thousand years before. Now, however, there were no strong, militaristic Chichimecs or Mixtecs to step in and take over. Mexico was splintered into irreconcilable factions during most of the nineteenth century; centralists fought federalists, conservatives fought liberals, Republicans fought Imperialists, even Yorkist and Scottish-rite Freemasons struggled for power. That, of course, is what makes democracy work. Not in Mexico, though. Here it produced an endless civil war. Finally two men appeared strong enough to put a stop to it, strong enough to grasp power, to hang onto it and use it to impose order on the prevailing chaos. Both were natives of Oaxaca: Benito Juárez and Porfirio Díaz.

Benito Juárez (1806-1872) was a pure-blooded Zapotec Indian who did not learn to speak Spanish until he was thirteen years old. Destined for the priesthood, he became a lawyer instead, a professor of law and the governor of Oaxaca. After that he occupied some of the highest federal posts during the stormy decade of the 1850's which ended with the Three Years' War, brought about by the promulgation of the Reform Laws of 1856 and 1857. In 1858 Mexico found itself without a head of state, and Juárez, as President of the Supreme Court, legally succeeded to the Presidency.

A series of financial and military crises following the Three Year's War culminated in the French Intervention and the Second Empire with Maximilian at its head. The country then split into Imperialists and Republicans. Juárez was on the run most of the time; gradually, his shabby black coach came to symbolize the patriotic heart of Mexico.

Meanwhile, Porfirio Díaz (1830-1915), a pupil and protegé of Juárez in Oaxaca, had joined the army and risen to the rank of Brigadier General. When the French left Maximilian to his fate, Porfirio Díaz mopped up the remaining Imperialist detachments in the south, starting with Tehuantepec and ending up in Mexico City, which he turned over, together with his army's funds, to Juárez's government.

The parting of the ways came with Juárez's re-election in 1870, after he had already been twelve years in the Presidency. Díaz rebelled against his old friend and mentor with the slogan, "no re-election!" Ironically, the Revolution which, after thirty years, tumbled him from power was sparked with the very same slogan.

Juárez and Díaz. Both proved to be precisely what Mexico needed at the time. Juárez saved the Republic, Díaz strengthened it. He pacified the country, bringing in foreign capital and expertise and opening the doors of Mexico to the Industrial Revolution. Juárez and Díaz started out as friends and ended up as bitter enemies; both became heroes in their own lifetimes. Juárez was saved from becoming a self-perpetuating dictator by a timely heart attack. Díaz, on the other hand, had a constitution so robust that he survived peritonitis in his twenties and the Revolution in his eighties — and Paris for four more years after that. Juárez planted the seeds of the agrarian revolt as early as 1858 by his expropriation of all corporate lands, including those of the Indian communities which were immediately grabbed by the hacendados with the tacit consent of Júarez's Liberal government. But since the Revolution, whose standard bearers still govern Mexico, was directed against Díaz, don Porfirio is condemned to eternal dishonor while Juárez's memory is honored in a heavenly choir of official canonization.

State of Guerrero: Acapulco (Náhuatl: *acatl*, reed, *pul*, augmentative particle, *co*, locative ending, "place of thick reeds.")

Acapulco's heraldic device should consist of a foaming wave on a field of azure bearing the motto: "It's been spoiled!" Spoiled or not, Acapulco contines to be Mexico's favorite resort. Hordes of honeymooners and holiday-makers rush lemming-like to Acapulco. They crowd onto beaches, sleeping on the sand, in campers, rooming houses or shoddy-expensive hotels. Back in Mexico City, they drop names of boutiques and nightclubs to prove that they have been to Acapulco. They haven't really, of course. The real Acapulco, the one that has fabricated the mystique of matchless hedonism throughout the world, the lemmings didn't even get a whiff of. It hovers in the blue air at an altitude of between 150 and 1000 feet above sea level, an altitude determined by the height of the most expensive penthouses and the villas with the grandest views. This Acapulco can only be reached on the big-money elevator or, if you are young, on the updrafts of warm and fragrant air that only beauty can generate.

Though Acapulco is no country for old men, the placed is packed with them. They have found there a Fountain of Youth. The old have the power, the young have the beauty: the two come together as inevitably as sex and money. The Fountain jets play wherever *the* party is going on. This is a continuous, free-floating event moving from villa to penthouse and back.

The habitué may protest. "I come here to rest. Acapulco is the most restful place in the world. I never go to parties, nor do any of my friends. We all live quietly. I seldom leave the house." You should see the house. If you are rich enough you can still build yourself a version of the unspoiled primeval garden. A villa floating like a cloud above the bay, a choice piece of water held in a marble shell and, behind the vistaed pool, a peristyle of fluted columns holding up a pediment of blue sky. Art and artifice can recreate some part of what the crowds and the higgledly-piggledy builders have spoiled. Without that kind of money, though, only a devotee of dawn and high purlieus may still catch a glimpse of Acapulco's fabled beauty.

The Asia Route

Acapulco's present vogue has obscured its historical importance. Forty years after the Conquest, it became the Spanish Empire's gateway to the Orient and to its South American colonies. The discovery by Fray Andrés de Urdañeta of the safe and easy return route from the Philippines marked the beginning of the China trade. The Manila Galleon connected the Spanish merchants of Seville with the Spice Islands (the Moluccas). The footpath connecting Mexico and Puebla with Acapulco came to be known as "the Asia Route," and the Puebla merchants dealing with both Veracruz and Acapulco, as the "*Mercaderes de Ambos Mares*," Merchants of Both Seas.

The market that took place in Acapulco in January, after the arrival of the Manila Galleon, became famous as "The Trade Fair of America," since it supplied the markets of Guatemala, Panama, Peru and Chile as well as those of Spain and New Spain. Acapulco became a babel during the fair. The Creole and Spanish merchants could not have understood a word said by the Japanese, Hindu, Malaysian and Chinese traders. The atmosphere of the port became as exotic as the silks, ivories, porcelains and spices that were its stock in trade. The fair generally ended up with a mock funeral that signalled the beginning of the pre-Lenten carnival celebration.

Inevitably, the freebooters arrived. The Dutch and English pirates who plagued the cities of the Spanish Main now turned their attention to the Pacific coast. In 1615 six vessels belonging to the Dutch East India Company entered the bay, though at the first cannon shots from land, the commanding officer hoisted the white flag. They exchanged their Spanish prisoners for fresh provisions. The experience led to the construction of the Fort of San Diego which, with substantial later modifications, still stands.

Tasco (Náhuatl: *Tlachco* – "(in) the ball game")

The Asia Route was no more than a footpath negotiable only by the Indian *tamemes* (porters) until 1592, when the Viceroy Luis de Velasco II (builder of the Alameda in Mexico City) made it suitable for pack mules. During the dry winter months, the trip took twelve days; during the summer rains, traffic practically came to a standstill. Nothing more was done about the road until 1750, when a silver millionaire by the name of José de la Borda improved the stretch between Tasco and Cuernavaca.

The Tasco mines – tin and iron as well as gold and silver – had been in continuous exploitation since pre-Hispanic times. The big silver strikes came in the eighteenth century, and the lode found by José de la Borda was one of the richest of all. When he broadened and repaired the road to Cuernavaca, he was at the peak of his prosperity. His fortune was such that he also undertook the reconstruction of the ruined parish church of Santa Prisca, which for many now stands as the perfect example of the Mexican Churrigueresque. There are many fine houses in Tasco. Humboldt thought it the only decent city in the province (Acapulco he characterized as "miserable"). Stately as some of the surrounding houses are, however, Borda's among them, none can be mentioned in the same breath as the crisp and fancifully elegant Santa Prisca.

The gleam of silver shines throughout the history of Tasco. A school of silversmiths developed that made "Tasco" a household word throughout Spain. Santa Prisca's silver treasure was particularly sumptuous. Most of it did not belong to the church, however. The canny Borda had only lent it to the parish, keeping the chalice, crowns and candelabra as security against a rainy day. When his first mine gave out, and his first fortune came to an end, he still had these objects in reserve. A single monstrance sold to the Mexico City Cathedral fetched 110,000 pesos in 1762. With that, and a lucky strike into the *Veta Grande* (Mother Lode) of Zacatecas, he was able to restore his fortune. He died in Cuernavaca, a rich man, in the gardens he had built for his retirement and which still bear his name.

Chilpancingo may be the state capital, but Acapulco is the cynosure, the center of attention. In 1765 a royal auditor discovered that the Viceroy, the Marquess of Cruillas, was heading a smuggling operation in Acapulco; at the turn of the century a Porfirian governor, Antonio Mercenario, fully justified his name during his term in power. The viceregal smuggler was immediately recalled, the mercenary governor was struck off the government payroll. A recent governor has been accused of every crime in the book. But nothing is done about it. That is the difference between the past and the present.

Acapulco, meanwhile, grows apace, sending out feelers along the Costa Grande to the north. The Acapulco mystique has established beach-heads all along the littoral, in Ixtapa-Zihuantanejo, and beyond the state boundaries into Michoacán and Colima, where the oceanic spaces are brought up short by embankments and stockades of palm forests. Near Manzanillo it reappears in the brilliant domed Casbah of Las Hadas, in the luxury of the quiet clubs and the extroversion of Mediterranées dotting the mangrove inlets north of Tenacatita, past Costa Careyes to Puerto Vallarta, where the steep hills open up to let the river waters pour out into the enormous Bahía de Banderas (Bay of Flags). The tendrils of Acapulco are now reaching beyond Vallarta to the other fortified Spanish port of the Pacific coast, San Blas, from which Alaska was discovered. They skirt the medallion-shaped island city of Mexcaltitan, only to plunge into the everglades and estuaries of southern Sinaloa and surface once more in Mazatlán. The Acapulco mystique has created the longest Côte d'Azur in the world, but this one has real sand, not pebbles, on the beach. It is the Pleasure Strand of the Pacific.

Morelos

The state of Morelos lies on the sun-washed southern slope of the Valley of Mexico. It is countryside of gradually descending valleys, of rich soils and deep ravines, and a vegetation that luxuriates in its perpetual spring. Even the names of its two principal cities, Cuernavaca and Cuautla, relfect the *luxe, calme et volupté* of the climate and the vegetation. Cuautla, from the Náhuatl, *cuahuitl*, tree, with the

133

collective -tla ending, means a woodland. Cuernavaca is merely the Spaniard's "horn and cow" (*cuerno y vaca*) corruption of the difficult Cuauhnáhuac, meaning, "near the trees."

Morelos became an independent federal state in 1869. It was named after José María Morelos, the octoroon priest who became the leader of the Insurgency after the execution of Miguel Hidalgo. His audacious break out of Cuautla, when it was beseiged by the Royalist army, was a crucial triumph in the War of Independence. A child of the Enlightenment – he called himself "the bondslave of the nation" – he convoked the First Constitutional Assembly in Chilpancingo in 1813. The egalitarian, republican manifesto issued the following year declared the sovereignty of all the people; "No Creoles or Castes," Morelos had said, "we are all Americans." This document is considered the forerunner of all our subsequent constitutions.

Like Miguel Hidalgo, Morelos was finally captured, tried, defrocked and shot. Maximilian raised a statue in his honor fifty years after his execution, and only one year before he himself had to face Juárez's firing squad.

Cuernavaca is to Morelos what Acapulco is to Guerrero: the center of gravity. It has been a lordly town since pre-Hispanic times. It became positively opulent under gardens Cortés and the Franciscan builders who followed him into the valley. In 1865 Maximilian, seduced by the exotic nature of the place, took over the dilapidated Borda gardens and endeavored to restore them to their original splendor. In that last and bitterest winter of his empire, he wrote, "Here we lead a really tropical life, surrounded by handsome, friendly and loyal natives." He was whistling in the dark. His government was bankrupt, his own health was failing, Napoleon III was pulling out stakes. Carlota wrote to him from Chapultepec: "I am glad you are happy in your earthly paradise, but, for me, there is no longer any paradise on earth."

Carlota fed on bitterness and jealousy during those final months before she lost her reason. Maximilian had fallen into the most common trap that time can set for the middle-aged man. As his vigor declined, he felt obliged to put on the airs of a Lothario. In Cuernavaca he went further. Dreaming away in his garden retreat, heedless of Juárez and his republican supporters, he had an affair with the wife of one of his gardeners. The rumor that she bore him a child is by all accounts false, though a man affecting his manner and claiming to be his son appeared in Europe during the First World War, and was shot by the French as a spy.

Cortés's Capital City

As recently as 1930, Cuernavaca was still the town in which the rich built their pleasure domes, while Acapulco, long fallen from the vigor of its Manila Galleon days, remained a huddle of quite remarkable undistinction. Now, of course, Acapulco has soared to the heights of touristic fame while Cuernavaca has become practically a suburb of Mexico City.

In pre-Hispanic times the population runoff from the valley – the late-comers, the weak, the unsuccessful – always spilled over toward the south and settled in the mild verdant region under the volcano. But a good climate and luxuriant vegetation also attract the powerful, and the warlords duly arrived, subdued the locals and exacted tribute from them. Many tribes succeeded one another in this fashion. A venerable Toltec legend relates that when the god Quetzalcóatl forsook eternity in order to enter worldly time, the incarnation took place in a virgin's womb and his birth as man took place in a valley to the east of Cuernavaca. The Aztec emperor Ahuízotl built the Tepozteco temple in his honor, on a cliff above the valley of Tepoztlán – not to be confused with Tepotzotlán, in the state of Mexico. The excellent quality of the cotton produced in these valleys had originally attracted the

Aztecs who conquered the local Tlahuicas in 1396.

Cortés first became aware of these valley cultures in 1521, while preparing for the siege of Tenochtitlán. He had sent an expedition to identify the Aztec cities immediately to the south. When it returned badly mauled, he personally headed a second expedition, unexpectedly approaching Cuernavaca from the south-east, which the natives had considered sufficiently protected by natural obstacles. The ravine of Amanalco cut Cortés off from the fortified city of Cuauhnáhuac like a moat. The city seemed unassailable until his Tlaxcalan allies found an *amate* tree, an immense wild ficus whose great boughs overhung the ravine, allowing them to drop safely on the far side.

The Cuernavaca Municipal Codex relates that the natives, seeing the strange armored men approaching from the direction of the supposedly unbridgeable *barranca*, took fright and fled north "toward Santa María." Leaving a detachment in charge, Cortés returned to Lake Texcoco and launched the siege that ended with the downfall of Tenochtitlán. It was a lightning campaign. He left the valley on 5 April, took Cuernavaca on the 13th and Tenochtitlán four months later, on 13 August, 1521.

When Cortés received the title of Marquess of the Valley of Oaxaca in 1529, he made Cuernavaca the capital city of his fief. He had already built himself a palace there – the same which now houses a museum and has some excellent murals, including *trompe l'oeil* furniture, by Diego Rivera. Cortés's second wife spent most of her time there. She was a peninsular aristocrat of unimpeachable lineage, and she preferred the sunny loggia overlooking the valley to the cold Coyoacán mansion where the Conquistador's first wife had died of poisoning. Cortés was accused of her murder and stood trial. The Court, the Second Audiencia (the good one), and even the dead woman's mother, ended up by agreeing that the charge was groundless.

Since 1523 Cortés had successfully grown sugar cane in the valley. His son, Martín, continued producing sugar after the Conquistador's death. The report of stupendous profits attracted many Spaniards but, as most of the land in the region belonged to the Marquesado and the convent it had endowed, the newcomers had to lease or buy from the Crown. They had no way to expand other than by "buying" or otherwise encroaching on the Indian communities' lands, which were inalienable by law. Later, the Reform Laws of 1857 legalized the purchase of these lands, which played straight into the hacendados' hands and left the communities destitute. Some growers even ploughed up the village streets to plant cane for their mills. The villagers had scant recourse to law, and in any case, could not expect to find a sympathetic ear with the state government, since it was hand-picked by Díaz from among his hacendado friends.

Emiliano Zapata (1879-1919)

Such were the conditions in which Zapata grew up. Anencuilco, his native village, was one of those whose streets had been ploughed up for sugar cane. By 1900 most Indian communities found themselves without a scrap of land in which to plant their maize. When apprised of this situation, one hacendado suggested that they plant it in flowerpots. The suggestion is strikingly reminiscent of Marie Antoniette's, "Let them eat cake." What followed in both cases was a revolution which permanently overthrew the landed aristocracy and deprived it of political power.

Zapata's open rebelliousness landed him in the army. There, his superb horsemanship caught the eye of President Díaz's son-in-law, who gave him a job looking after his thoroughbreds. After a few months he returned to Anencuilco, where the community elected him president and entrusted him with the defense and recovery of their lands, whose titles dated from pre-Hispanic times and had been ratified by the Spanish Crown.

When the Revolution broke out, Zapata threw in his lot with Madero, insisting on the inclusion of a plank on agrarian reform in Madero's platform, which was a purely political one of "effective suffrage and no re-election." In the skirmishes, guerilla raids and head-on battles of the Revolution, Zapata proved invincible. A total identification of purpose with the Indians and dispossessed peasants of Morelos gave him a strength beyond numbers and logistics. He became a force of nature, cutting through the sectarianism that finally destroyed Madero's Revolution. His virtuosity on horseback earned him the name of "the Centaur of the South" even as Pancho Villa came to be known as "the Centaur of the North." Obsessed by the need of agrarian reforms, he quarrelled with every revolutionary leader. After breaking with the Constitutionalist President Carranza, Zapata and Pancho Villa took Mexico City.

The terrified citizenry barricaded itself against "Attila's hordes." Nothing happened. Indians in coarse white drawers and enormous peaked hats wandered shyly around the city, still carrying their guns but meekly asking for directions. They disappeared as quietly as they arrived.

Finding Zapata invincible in the field, Carranza sent him a Trojan Horse, a fake defector from the Constitutionalist army. Laboriously he earned Zapata's trust, taking government garrisons and even executing hostages. One day he invited Zapata to have lunch with him. Zapata arrived with a small escort at his hacienda headquarters. The buglers greeted him with fanfares, a guard of honor presented arms. As the last note sounded, the guards shouldered their muskets and fired pointblank into Zapata's chest.

Zapata's death has saved all subsequent agrarian leaders and governments a lot of embarassment. In his name, politicians have transformed his ideal into an inexhaustible honeypot. His Plan de Ayala of 1911, which embodied his agrarian ideas, demanded the return of "usurped" lands to "the towns or individuals having the respective titles to the properties." Such a program, had it been implemented, would have returned autonomy to the Indian communities along with their land, creating at the same time a large class of small landowners such as Juárez's Reform Laws had envisaged when they outlawed corporate ownership of the land.

Diego Rivera's murals-with-a-message are about as exhilarating as an editorial in an Albanian daily. One marvels only at his utter lack of embarassment in wielding the most transparent clichés. But when he stops preaching and starts feeling, he stands revealed as a painter of genius. He is at his strongest when dealing with the realm of nature. When he portrays man living in the natural order of things, he transcends politics and creates an existential cosmos of unique beauty. The Mexican landscape moved Rivera to reveal a symbolic truth nourished by passion. In his mural depicting the crossing of the Almanalco gorge by Cortés and his allies, his scantily clad Tlaxcalans swarm erotically over the pale, thick boughs of the *amate*. They embrace those branches over the dark chasm with all their love of life, while their friends on the near side stand among the foliage holding the branches fast by their tips.

Zapata cannot be held responsible for the torrents of dishonest rhetoric and the tons of maimed sculpture executed in his name. His lumpy equestrian likenesses stand facing every agricultural valley in the country. Only one monument does Zapata justice: the effigy Rivera painted on the chapel walls of the former Hacienda of Chapingo, now the National School of Agriculture. There the dead crusader lies, in a coffin hollowed out of the earth, wrapped in the blood-stained shroud of a murdered man. The roots of the field are growing down through the earth into his niche to tap his strength. Zapata slumbers in the earth he loved, beyond the injustices he abhorred.

85

84. *Chamula (Chiapas). Tzotzil Indian women bottling the local spirit, distilled from the* agave.

85. *Palenque (Chiapas). The Temple of Inscriptions, Classic Maya.*

86. *Palenque (Chiapas). Aerial view, showing the Palace on the left and the Temple of the Inscriptions on the right. Since this Maya city was abandoned in the tenth century AD the jungle has gradually engulfed it. The area so far uncovered (about 550 yards by 300) represents only a fraction of the site, which may well extend for several miles into the forest.*

87

87. *Palenque (Chiapas). The Palace. This is really a group of buildings and courtyards with a central tower, constructed in successive stages on the site of older buildings. It stands on a huge artificial platform, and is approached from the front by a great staircase 208 feet wide.*

88. *On the road between Monte Albán and Oaxaca (Oaxaca). A shepherd with his sheep, wearing a plastic sheet to keep off the rain — a dubious innovation which replaces the traditional thatched cape.*

89. *Tenejapa (Chiapas). A Chamula Indian in traditional dress.*

90. *Monte Albán (Oaxaca). General view of this spectacular pre-Columbian site, which lies at about 6,500 feet above sea level. Zapotec culture, 100-900 AD.*

88

89

91. *Tlacolula (Oaxaca). An Indian traveler pausing at the foot of a cross.*

92. *Monte Albán (Oaxaca). Monumental wall of a building along the east side of the central square. Zapotec culture, 100-900 AD.*

93. *Oaxaca. Wax figure in an original Indian mask and bearing a gourd, in the museum of the Monastery of Santo Domingo.*

94. *Santa María del Tule, near Oaxaca (Oaxaca). The trunk of a two thousand-year-old cypress. It is 130 feet high, and measures 138 feet round the base and is presumed by many to be the oldest living thing in the world.*

95. *View of curving land formations on the coast near Salina Cruz (Oaxaca).*

96. *Acapulco (Guerrero). View of a swimming pool with fake waves, fake whale, and painted border, with the Bay of Acapulco in the background.*

97. *The rapids at Agua Azul, near Palenque (Chiapas). The water here is exceptionally clear and it is a favorite place for bathing.*

98. *View of the mountains surrounding Oaxaca City, taken from Monte Albán.*

97

98

99. Oaxaca. Cloister of the Monastery of Santo Domingo, built by the Dominicans between 1550 and 1600. The cloister was rebuilt in the early seventeenth century.

100. Xochicalco (Morelos). The Pyramid of the Plumed Serpents, which seems to have been erected to commemorate a gathering of astronomer-priests at which some correction was made to the Aztec calendar. On its sloping walls are bas-reliefs of eight plumed serpents (two on each side). Xochicalco was inhabited as early as the fifth century AD, and enjoyed its period of greatest importance from the seventh to tenth centuries.

101. Xochicalco (Morelos). Bas-relief carvings on the wall of the Pyramid of the Plumed Serpents (detail of no. 100).

102

103

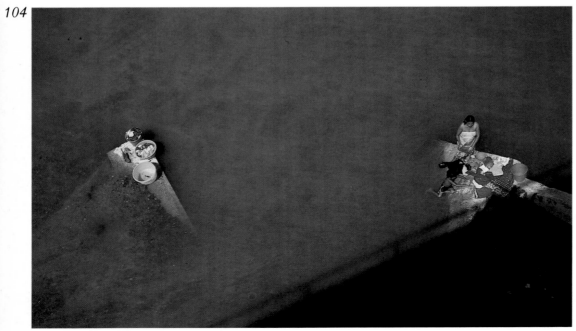

104

102. *Tlacolula (Oaxaca). Working in the heat of mid-day.*

103. *Tlacochahuaya (Oaxaca). House wall in mud and brick in the early morning light.*

104. *Río Omitlán (Guerrero). Woman doing her washing in the river.*

105. *Santa Astata (Oaxaca). The painted facade of the church with the ox-cart and oxen that are still a familiar feature of the Mexican scene.*

106

106. *Teposcolula (Oaxaca). Basket-work in the main square.*

107. *Village scene in Zinacantan (Chiapas). Cloth-weaving on a traditional frame.*

108. *Tlacolula (Oaxaca). Street scene in a small Zapotec town.*

109. *Chenalho (Chiapas). Musicians playing typical forms of guitar and harp in a private house.*

107

108

109

155

110. *Cuernavaca (Morelos). The Palace of Cortés, probably begun in 1532, but altered by Cortés's son and again in the nineteenth century. In the foreground, a pre-Hispanic monolith.*

111. *Coixtlahuaca (Oaxaca). Cloister of the Dominican monastery, one of the most impressive in Mexico, founded in 1544.*

112. *Mitla (Oaxaca). The richly decorated facade of one of the temples on this site, probably belonging to the Mixtec culture although the city was inhabited by the Zapotecs when the Spaniards arrived.*

113

114

113. *Cuilapan (Oaxaca). The "open chapel,"*
which is in fact the ruined (and roofless) basilica
of one of the largest monasteries in New Spain,
begun by the Dominicans in about 1548.

114. *Teposcolula (Oaxaca). Columns and*
arches of the ruined "open chapel." Constructed
towards 1570, and originally surmounted by a
cupola, this building is interesting particularly
for its concessions to the Gothic style in a
Renaissance framework.

115. *Tasco (Guerrero). A street scene in this*
charming, typically colonial town, with the bell
tower of Santa Prisca in the distance.

Chapter 4
The Heartland: El Centro

The States of Mexico, Hidalgo, Querétaro, Guanajuato, Zacatecas, Aguascalientes, Durango, San Luis Potosí, Michoacán, Colima, Jalisco, Nayarit.

These states comprise the quintessential Mexico, with its double-rooted past and its present coat of many colors. By comparison, the south seems too idiosyncratic, too close to its non-Mexican, pre-Hispanic roots, while the north is too rootless, to prone to veer away into the irresistible orbit of the United States.

In this central region we find the living reality of our three cultures. Native populations live in their original communities, and in countless country markets you are likely to hear as much Otomí and Náhuatl as Spanish. The Creoles have also traditionally gravitated toward certain regions like the highlands (*los altos*) of Jalisco where their high coloring and fair complexion emphasize their European features. And throughout one finds the Mestizos, the most numerous group in the country, the ones who, in the final analysis, keep Mexico more or less fuelled and in working order.

In no other region can we find a richer or more varied collection of pre-Hispanic and Spanish Colonial monuments. The heartland illustrates the continuity of our pre-Hispanic culture, on the one hand, and, on the other, the wild variety of colonial invention which has resulted from the mixture of Spanish and Indian sensibilities. Geographically, it resembles the landlocked provinces of central Spain: wide, tawny plains, valleys clenched in mountains and watered by the headstreams that flow down to irrigate the plains along either coast. The churches with their cupolas, the fortress convents and the fortified haciendas scattered about the arid landscape intensify the Castilian atmosphere. The cities San Miguel de Allende, Querétaro, Zacatecas, and Morelia would not look out of place in Castile or Aragón. Yet the same bend in the road might just as easily take you to the heart of pre-Hispanic Teotenango, or to one of those wide, stepped-back truncated cones improbably termed "round pyramids," or again to a monolithic temple complex like Malinalco's.

The heartland also provides a summary of Mexican history. Our economy was forged in its mines and haciendas. Our religion was carried to the furthest marches of the land, first by Spanish missionaries, then by their Indian and Mestizo disciples. The independent republic was born here, midwifed by Creole intellectuals and officers of the royalist army. The heartland cities held out against the French invasion and Maximilian's empire. Both Querétaro and San Luis Potosí were at one time or another capitals of the embattled republic.

Such volume and diversity of material clearly requires special organization, which will be based on the principal cultural divisions found here by the Spaniards at the time of the Conquest.

To the north of Tenochtitlán extended the enormous territory of the *Gran Chichimeca*, a country occupied by tribes of nomadic hunters. To the west, the *Cultura de Occidente* fanned out to the Pacific Coast, covering the present states of Michoacán, Colima, Jalisco, Nayarit and snippets of all the states around them. The outlanders living closest to Tenochtitlán were the most civilized: the Otomíes of Otumba, immediately north on the border of the Gran Chichimeca; the Tarascan Kingdom of Michoacán directly to the west, which forms part of the Cultura de Occidente. The Indians of the more remote regions were the most indomitable. It took the forty-year Chichimeca War to subdue the Guachichiles of San Luis Potosí, while the even more remote Coras of the sierra in Nayarit were still unsubdued a hundred years ago.

The Gran Chichimeca and the Cultura de Occidente, then, will be the principal divisions of this chapter.

La Gran Chichimeca

Once the Aztec Empire was sufficiently under control, Cortés, helped by his old and new allies, turned his attention to the north. The Franciscans were his most effective troops. They presently learned as much as any foreigner could about the local cultures. Some became linguists, like Fray Alonso de Medina, who wrote the first Náhuatl-Spanish dictionary, which is still a standard reference book. Another, Fray Francisco de Tembleque, turned out to be an architectural genius. Seeing the natives of Otumba drinking out of the same stagnant pools as the encomendero's horses and cattle, he conceived the idea of bringing fresh water in from Zempoala, 45 kilometers away, an awesome project on such broken terrain. With the help of several thousand Indians, and no technical knowledge beyond his common sense and intuition, he finished the work in seventeen years.

Meanwhile, a large floating population developed, consisting of ex-soldiers, prospectors, new arrivals, all trying in the best picaresque tradition to make their dreams of riches come true. Some went crazy, burrowing into the northern mountains, following the glint of stone seen in an Indian's hand, or ambiguous, murmured directions. Others, as we shall see, were luckier.

State of Mexico (Náhuatl, *Mexictli*, "In the navel of the moon," from *metzli*, moon, and *xictli*, navel). Capital: Toluca (Náhuatl, *tolocan*, "Place of those who bow their heads," from *toloa*, to bow or nod).

Since Classic times central Mexico has undoubtedly been the premier province of the country. On its soil grew three of the sovereign civilizations of Mesoamerica, the Teotihuacán, the Toltec and the Aztec, each supremely powerful in its own day. The Aztec civilization looms larger than the others because it is closer to us in time, and because the Spanish Conquest caught and preserved it in the apogee of its power and splendor. There is little reason to believe, though, that it was in any way superior to those that preceded it.

New Spain was divided into twenty-three major provinces. Five of them – Mexico, Tlaxcala, Puebla, Antequera (Oaxaca) and Valladolid (Michoacán) – formed the Reign of Mexico. Three provinces each formed the Reign of New Galicia and the Governorship of Yucatán, and the remaining twelve provinces constituted the so-called Internal Provinces of the North. This jumble of judicatures was created by the Spanish Hapsburgs (*los Austrias*) and soon degenerated into an administrative chaos which the eighteenth-century Bourbon kings of Spain regarded with Cartesian distaste and set about putting in order. Overcoming the opposition of the conservative and very Spanish viceroys, they reorganized the country into twelve intendancies by means of which they standardized institutions and procedures under a central authority and thereby achieved unprecedented efficiency.

Under the new dispensation, the Intendancy of Mexico kept its primacy because it continued to house the viceroy, the army, and the Audiencia (the supreme tribunal that assumed executive power in the absence of the viceroy). The Intendancy consisted of Mexico City and the present states of Mexico, Hidalgo, Morelos and Guerrero. In 1824, the First Constitutional Congress of the independent republic sheared off the Federal District from the territory of the erstwhile intendancy, which was at the same time declared a federal state. In the same year, the new state held its own Constitutional Assembly in the old Palace of the Inquisition.

After the 1824 Constitution, the State of Mexico reflected the chaotic conditions of the country as a whole. During the centralist interregnum of 1835-46, the State of Mexico became a department which included the Federal District and the former State of Tlaxcala. With the restoration of federalism in 1846, all the states went back to their former boundaries. But in 1849, after the American war, the State of Mexico lost a great deal of its territory with the creation of the State of Guerrero, which extended practically from Cuernavaca to Acapulco. During a brief return to centralism in 1853, the "district" of Morelos was organized within the revived

Department of Mexico. Then, during the French Intervention, the State of Mexico was split up into three military districts, which in 1869, after the restoration of the republic, turned into the separate states of Mexico, Hidalgo and Morelos.

The State of Mexico, then, reduced from its former exalted situation, suddenly found itself in possession of some of the poorest soil but many of the finest monuments, both pre-Hispanic and of the old colonial Intendancy, very much like Yucatán after it lost Campeche and Quintana Roo. This woeful tale of mutilation, however, ends unexpectedly on an optimistic note. Whereas Yucatán has yet to recover from its mutilation, Mexico has in recent years developed into one of the richest states in the republic simply because of its proximity to Mexico City. The state surrounds the Federal District on three sides, enfolding also much of Morelos to the south, and therefore holds the country's richest market cupped within its boundaries.

State boundaries are a recent and arbitrary political convention. The old civilizations were organic growths that expressed the needs of man and society in a given land. Geographically, their limits had no relation to our modern state boundaries, so it makes sense to discuss them all together now, simply to fix them chronologically and geographically in the reader's mind.

The over-restored remains of Teotihuacán, the "City of the Gods" which dominated most of the Classic period in northern Mesoamerica, stand in what is now the State of Mexico. Tula, the capital of the Toltecs, who prevailed in the Early Post-Classic (900-1200), is in the State of Hidalgo.

Teotihuacán, Tula and Malinalco

A panoramic view of Mexico is not the place for a detailed examination of our archeological past, which, moreover, has been studied in depth in countless books. For this purpose, a snapshot must suffice. In Teotihuacán, for example, one should know that the Pyramid of the Moon antedates the Pyramid of the Sun. This suggests that the original Teotihuacanos may have been part of a matriarchal, moon-worshiping culture. If so, the building of the much larger Pyramid of the Sun would represent the displacement of the matriarchate by the patriarchal, sun-worshiping society. The later Aztec pictograph for Tenochtitlán, now Mexico's national emblem, may be its most definitive expression.

The name Quetzalcóatl, besides "Plumed Serpent" also means "precious – or divine – twin," quetzal feathers being considered precious, of divine origin, while twin is a secondary meaning of *cóatl*, serpent. Among starworshipers, Quetzalcóatl, the divine twin, meant the planet Venus in its twin aspect as morning and evening star.

The Quetzalcóatl cult from Teotihuacán did not become a man-god legend until the appearance of the messiah-like Ce-Acatl-Topiltzin, who founded the Toltec capital at Tula. This human leader, who assumed the name of the god Quetzalcóatl, advocated the end of the ritual wars and of human sacrifice. This bringer of light left his followers but promised to return. And return he did. Some found him in the Spanish Conquistador, others in the missionaries' Christ. But long before that he had already made good his cosmic promise, for he daily reappeared as the divine twin, the morning star heralding the sun and, in the darkling sky, the evening star guiding the sun over the rim of night.

Quetzalcóatl was generally identified with the morning star while his evening twin was transmogrified into a dog-headed god known as Xólotl. Xólotl was also the name for the Pame-Chichimec chieftain who ultimately destroyed Tula, the city that had expelled Quetzalcóatl. This earthly Xólotl (1244-1304) achieved great power. He led his Chichimecs into the central valley, where he built the core of what is now the wondrous seven-shelled pyramid of Tenayuca, a model for the later Aztec builders.

Of the divine twins, Xólotl has had a more curious and specific afterlife than Quetzalcóatl. The latter remained the Plumed Serpent, the former became a fat little hairless dog, the "Xólotl-*itzcuintli*" which guides men's souls into the realm of the dead as the evening star guides the dying sun. The *xóloizcuintle*, as he is now called, is the most amiable of creatures. We will run across him further on, in the pit-and-chamber burial vaults of *Occidente*, his polished red ceramic image still keeping the bones of his master company.

A novel architectural development of the Late Post-Classic was the carving of monuments in living rock. In Malinalco, the Aztecs achieved the most remarkable results in this technique of what is essentially monolithic sculpture. They carved a hillside of solid rock into a series of terraces, staircases, temples and even a round sanctuary, adorned with relief carvings of jaguars and eagles, emblems of the Aztecs' knightly military orders.

State of Hidalgo (Named after Miguel Hidalgo y Costilla) Capital: Pachuca (Náhuatl, *Pachyocan*, "a narrow place," from the verb *pachoa*, to press or to oppress).

A mine, a convent, a hacienda. Based upon this trinity, the life of New Spain gradually took shape; they existed all over New Spain, though the heartland states are possibly the region where they reached their most distinctive expression. In Hidalgo, the silver mine of Real del Monte, the Augustinian convent of Actopan, and the pulque hacienda of San Antonio Ometusco are the exemplars.

The Mine: Real del Monte

Zacatecas, Hidalgo and Guanajuato are the earliest significant mining centers established after the Conquest. The first silver strikes in Pachuca and nearby Real del Monte took place in 1552 and were so spectacular that the word "*pachocha*," a corruption of Pachuca, became in popular speech a slang synonym for wealth. What is known as the patio system of silver extraction by means of amalgamation with quicksilver was invented in Pachuca in 1555 by the Spaniard Bartolomé de Medina. This gave silver mining great impetus, but also made New Spain more dependent than ever on Spain because of its virtual monopoly on the production of quicksilver.

The first silver boom, which started with the Zacatecas strikes of 1548 followed by those of Guanajuato, Pachuca and Real del Monte in 1552, financed the exploration and settlement of the northern provinces, the development of Peru and the conquest of the Philippines. The second boom, which began in Real del Monte about 1740, financed the second – and greater – if less permanent – northward expansion, which more than doubled the territory of New Spain.

The first silver boom lasted less than a century. Its most productive mines had either been flooded or had gone too deep for profitable exploitation with the current technology. Mining then became a hit-or-miss prospecting affair, discovering thin lodes near the surface until a new breed of miner, determined to follow the mother lodes, appeared. One of these bought the flooded Vizcaína mines in Real del Monte with the idea that he could drain the mine not out of the top, as was the usual practice, but out of the bottom by aiming and boring a tunnel from the foot of the mountain to the foot of the mine shaft and letting the water run out of its own accord. The working of the tunnel produced enough silver on its own to finance the venture. After several years' work and at a distance of 2,352 meters from its mouth, the tunnel finally struck the Vizcaína mother lode, which made its owner, Pedro Romero de Terreros, such a rich man that, says Humboldt, "the estate he left his children has only been equalled in Mexico by that of the Conde de la Valenciana (Antonio de Obregón y Alcocer, owner of the Valenciana mine in Querétaro). Humboldt goes on to tell us that "apart from two men-of-war that he gave King Charles III, of which one had 112 cannons, he lent the Crown in Madrid one million pesos which have not yet been repaid." The loan was eventually repaid – in the fashion most favored by kings. In 1769, Pedro Romero de Terreros was given the title of Conde de Santa María de Regla without having to furnish evidence of the five requisites for nobility, evidence pertaining to religious orthodoxy and "purity" of blood. Such grand concessions do not come cheap.

Fanny Calderón, visiting Real del Monte in 1840, provides details of a more gossipy nature. "The whole country here, as well as the mines, formerly belonged to the Count of Regla, who was so wealthy that when his son, the father of the present Count, was christened, the whole party walked from his house to the church upon ingots of silver. The Countess, having quarreled with the Vicereyne, sent her in token of reconciliation a white satin slipper, entirely covered with large diamonds. The Count invited the King of Spain to visit his Mexican territories, assuring him that the hoofs of His Majesty's horse should touch nothing but solid silver from Veracruz to the capital." By shoeing His Majesty's horse in silver, one presumes.

Mexico's struggle for Independence had kept the country in turmoil between 1810 and 1821. The mines were abandoned and the mining industry subsided into a coma for the duration. Mexico's independence from Spain, however, suddenly made Mexican investments particularly attractive to other Europeans, especially the English. In 1824, Real del Monte stock was offered in London and suddenly a silver fever as acute as the tulip craze of the 1600's seized England. The Real del Monte bubble burst in 1848 after losing over one million pounds. The assets were bought in 1850 by the partnership of Escandón and Béistegui, who soon afterwards struck the spectacularly rich El Rosario lode which, within a few years, gave them close to eighty million dollars profit.

Mexico's mineral wealth backfired from the beginning. The first boom produced such inflation in Spain that wages rose 300% between 1550 and 1620, which left Spain defenseless against the cheaper and more abundant goods of northern Europe. Spain tried to protect itself in the mercantilist fashion of the times by establishing a hermetic monopoly on trade with its New World colonies and, in addition, by outlawing all industrial competition from the colonies themselves. New Spain, hampered in every effort to develop industrially, was forced to buy its manufactured goods from Spain with bullion. It lived off capital from the beginning and never learned to create a competitive capital-goods industry. And so, finding a mine or its equivalent – a buried treasure – became from the earliest times the national dream, beyond which the average Mexican mentality has not progressed. A lottery-of-life psychology developed which has closed, bolted and barred the door on anything like a national work ethic. The Virgin of Guadalupe or a lottery *cachito* (1/20 of a ticket) can make anyone of us a millionaire overnight. In Mexico, even the most successful buy reams of lottery tickets, which may be the peak of greediness, but is perhaps inevitable in a country whose prosperity has always depended on finding one more silver mine and ever more abundant oil fields.

The Convent: Actopan

If a traveler can visit only one colonial monument in Mexico, the knowledgeable agree that it should be the Augustinian convent of Actopan. It constitutes a compendium of the architectural idioms in use in the middle of the sixteenth century.

Since the Franciscans had arrived first, the Augustinians were forced to venture further afield. They went north to the Gran Chichimeca and west to the Tarascan Kingdom of Michoacán. Labor being scarce there, the Augustinians built less and more slowly than either the Franciscans in central Mexico or the Dominicans in the south. The important buildings they did put up, however, remain monuments to their high ambition. They built like city planners rather than architects, and their convent in Yuriria, Michoacán, for example, achieved majestic proportions.

Actopan, like most sixteenth-century convents in New Spain, illustrates the transition from the Gothic style to the round arch of the Plateresque, as the Renaissance style is called in Spain and its colonies. The cloister, for instance, has groined vaults and tall Gothic arches on the ground floor, while the floor above has double round arches over every pointed arch below. Originally, the light Gothic skeleton evolved out of the sturdy Romanesque body to capture the hesitant light of northern Europe. Now in the New World it faced two contrary stimuli: the stylistic change to the Neo-Romanesque of the Renaissance, and the hot summers and radiant skies, which clamored for smaller windows and a heavier building fabric. Throughout the sixteenth century, Gothic ribbings continued to appear in church interiors, though more for esthetic than for structural reasons. In the end, however, the round arch prevailed, with its correspondingly massive walls. The climate has the final say in all good building. The first Viceroy, Antonio de Mendoza, keenly aware of the importance of convents, thought it convenient to establish a set of rules regarding their architectural organization. Among the things he decreed was that all convents should be built facing west. So one must stand with one's back to the afternoon sun in order to appreciate the originality of Actopan. The vast mandatory atrium is still there, though the surrounding wall is not. Adjoining the church on its north side, and at the far end of the atrium, rises the huge arch of its open chapel, Mexico's unique contribution to ecclesiastical architecture. It was designed to accommodate the multitudes who thronged to Mass and could not be fitted inside the church. In the open chapel, Mass was said in the vernacular for their special benefit. The Actopan open chapel is a *tour de force* of engineering. Deceptively light in appearance, the span of its barrel vault measures 17.5 meters across, which makes it wider than the naves of Notre Dame in Paris, of Amiens, Toledo or Seville. It is three meters wider than the nave of the Actopan church itself, and made to look considerably bigger by its *trompe l'oeil* coffered ceiling. The cloister, aside from its Gothic-Renaissance hybrid character, has a further point of interest. The wide stair well has walls covered on all four sides by perfectly preserved black and white murals depicting genre scenes from the conventual life of the followers of Saint Augustine. These murals provide us with the fullest inventory of sixteenth-century objects and furnishings. The refectory to the south of the cloister has a coffered barrel vault similar to the one in the open chapel, though not on such a vast scale. It is much longer, but lower and narrower. The *trompe l'oeil* effect of the coffering is here so perfect that it takes a minute to realize that it is real coffering recessed into the fabric of the vault and painted there to suggest a *trompe l'oeil*. The doors and windows offer another delicious surprise. Cut diagonally through the massive masonry of the walls on an axis that crosses a corner of the room and goes out through another similarly biased door, these openings catch every breeze but will not allow a direct view into the room. This is functionalism of the highest order.

The Hacienda: San Antonio Ometusco

The first thing to know about Ometusco is that it is a pulque hacienda. Haciendas under other names — *fincas*, plantations, *cortijos* — exist throughout the world, but a pulque hacienda exists only in Mexico. And even in Mexico, only the central states produce pulque. This pre-Hispanic drink, fermented from the juice of the giant agave, enjoyed such extraordinary popularity that the Aztec lawgivers made pulque drinking a capital offense for all able-bodied men under the age of sixty. A first offender's hair was cropped; a second offender's house was razed to the ground; a man found drunk for the third time was sacrificed with his entire family. Yet pulque continued to be produced and secretly drunk. All sorts of myth and ritual surrounded pulque. The celebrants of the pulque cult had to be over sixty, of course. Their deity was a rabbit (*tochtli*, possibly the origin of the Náhuatl word for pulque, which is *octli*), ritually called *Ome Tochtli* ("Two-Rabbit") so that the word Ometusco is simply a corruption of *Ome Tochtli*, the god of drunkenness, making the hacienda, by its name alone, the archetype of all pulque haciendas.

The overgrazed soils of Apan, the wind-swept, hail-smitten plains of southern Hidalgo, are the favorite habitat of the *maguey*, as the pulque agave is known. The proximity of the Mexico City market, moreover, made the maguey the ideal crop for the local landowners. Between 1785 and 1789 it was the Crown's fourth most important source of revenue. In don Porfirio's time, especially after the arrival of the Veracruz-Mexico railroad, pulque haciendas became gilt-edged investments for the landed gentry, producing a low but steady income which could not be matched by the wheat, corn, beans or other crops which were vulnerable to pests, diseases and the frequent hailstorms of the area. In this affluent period, the "pulque aristocracy" joined the oligarchy of the silver aristocracy and the cattle barons of the north.

If the stuff was so "matchlessly horrible" one wonders today how pulque ever became so popular as to be the national drink. The answer may be found once again in the writings of Fanny Calderón de la Barca.

Puebla, 24 December 1839. On the route from Veracruz to Puebla, the *alcalde* of La Ventilla made them taste pulque. "I should regret to attempt describing the smell — the reverse of roses we may say ... I am afraid my look of horror must have given mortal offense to the worthy alcalde, who considers it the most delicious beverage in the world."

4 June 1840, San Fernando, Mexico. After describing a harrowing taking of the veil by a young aristocratic girl, she adds, "I had almost made up my mind to see no more such scenes — which, unlike pulque and bullfights, I dislike more and more upon trial ..."

30 March 1841, Hacienda of Goicoechea, San Angel. Calderón's mission has come to an end. They have put their house in the city up for sale and have retired to a friend's "unoccupied country house ... with a fine garden and orchard full of fruit, with pretty walks all through it, and a sort of underwood of roses and sweet peas. It is a great pulque hacienda." (Now, as most tourists know, it houses the elegant San Angel Inn Restaurant.) "I never experienced such perfect stillness. Even the barking of a dog sounds like an event ... the Indians come in the morning to drink pulque (which by the way, I now think excellent, and shall find it very difficult to live without)."

Querétaro and Guanajuato

Querétaro and Guanajuato are known together, with a fine disregard for originality but a strict respect for truth, as "The Cradle of our Independence." Nothing else in the area, not the prodigious lodes of La Valenciana, nor the vast haciendas, the gilded altars of Querétaro, nor the spectacular flowering of the Baroque with its stone facades, can match the importance of the Insurgency sparked by Miguel Hidalgo, the priest from Dolores, Guanajuato, and the Creole conspirators in Querétaro.

An Indian pueblo conquered in 1532, Querétaro was the older city. It flourished as a presidio-garrison town and trading post on the Zacatecas silver route as early as 1550. The discovery of the Guanajuato mines between 1552 and 1556 created a brisk additional demand and valley towns like San Miguel el Grande and Celaya prospered along with Querétaro. During the heavy eighteenth-century influx of immigrants from northern Spain, the Querétaro-Guanajuato economy reached its colonial peak. Merchants, textile manufacturers, hacendados and miners intermarried and invested in one another's ventures. Their obrajes (textile mills), their haciendas, their mines were the richest and best managed in Mexico. The merchants held the purse strings to all these ventures, gradually becoming investment bankers as well as traders. Members of the silver aristocracy went to the merchants for cash, discovered new lodes so that both parties became fabulously rich, like Obregón (a miner) and Otero (a merchant), whom the Valenciana mine made, according to Humboldt, the richest men in the world.

The Conspiracy of Martín Cortés (1565-1568)

A powerful society of self-made men invariably rebels against colonial status. The first, unsuccessful, example of this phenomenon occurred in New Spain shortly after the Conquest; its leaders were the sons of Cortés and his captains. It must be kept in mind that the Conquest, like other early ventures of that sort, was a result of private enterprise on the part of the conquistadors, so they looked on their encomiendas as the spoils of war. They had risked their lives and fortunes for them, while the Crown had risked nothing. The encomenderos could hardly know that the Crown felt their power in New Spain as a threat to its sovereignty. The New Laws of 1542 were the Crown's first step in the demolition of the nascent feudalism in New Spain. The Mendicant Friars cheered, but the encomenderos howled and decided to secede from Spain and to establish their own monarchy in the New World. They chose as their leader Martín Cortés, the son of the Conquistador, newly arrived from the Spanish court and invested with the glamour of being Philip II's friend. Given a royal welcome by the Viceroy Luis de Velasco, Martín Cortés immediately antagonized him. The conspirators applauded and became rasher by the minute. They discussed their plot openly and swaggered before the Crown officials. Their insolence became a public scandal.

They did not have long to wait for an answer. Martín Cortés was easily flattered into the first trap laid for him. Arrested as he arrived at the Audiencia's offices in the viceregal palace, he was accused of treason and put in prison together with the principal conspirators. Some were summarily executed. Martín Cortés and his half-brothers were sent to Spain to stand trial. Though his estate, sequestered by the Crown in 1567, was returned in 1574, Martín never returned to New Spain.

The Mexican Enlightenment

This aborted conspiracy only confirmed the defeat inflicted by Charles V on the comunidades in 1521. The Crown became increasingly powerful. It created *corregimientos* – Crown encomiendas – to govern all free townships and cities while the private encomienda system was being dismantled. It also supported the secular clergy against the regular clergy, whose immense influence with the natives represented another threat to the power of the Crown. Peninsular clergy, considered more trustworthy than Creoles, Indians or Mestizos, received most preferments, and the Jesuits, whose company was created to counteract the disintegrating effect of the Reformation, were sent to New Spain in 1572, where they established the most influential school system to date.

During the first 150 years in New Spain, the Jesuits became the mentors of the ruling class. They built great colleges and established missions in the most ungrateful outposts of the Sonora and California deserts. In the course of the eighteenth century, however, they did an intellectual about-face that would have pained their founder as much as it pained their monarch. A large number of Central European Jesuits volunteered for missionary work in Mexico. They arrived trailing the heady ideas of the Enlightenment in their wake. They taught their students, the brilliant young Miguel Hidalgo among them, to read Rousseau and the Philosophes . . . and to think for themselves. Debating clubs sprang up under the guise of "literary societies." Short-lived newspapers spread the infection that began to pose a serious threat to the authority of the monarchy. Charles III decided to act. Being an enlightened despot — that is, the only man in the realm who can hold enlightened views without being subversive — he decided to get rid of the Jesuits. In 1767 he expelled the Company of Jesus from Spain and its dominions by a ban reading: "Let it be known by the following that the subjects of His Majesty, King of Spain, were born to be silent and to obey in silence and not to discuss and express opinions on the high affairs of the government." Free thought, however, is more addictive than any alkoloid, and the Jesuits' influence was irreversible. The Jesuits had trained several generations to think for themselves, and they became an irresistible force in public opinion. Conspiracies proliferated in various provincial capitals, inspired first by the American and then by the French Revolutions. The Rights of Man replaced the Apostle's Creed.

Miguel Hidalgo y Costilla (1753-1811)

The power vacuum in Spain set the viceregal edifice trembling, such unstable times seemed made to order for the parish priest of Dolores, Miguel Hidalgo y Costilla, one of the most independent and idiosyncratic men ever born. Having great talent and small means, he chose to study for the priesthood as the surest means of advancement for a young man of his type. He studied with the Jesuits in Valladolid (now Morelia, in Michoacán) where his genius in Latinity and Scholastic Theology was rewarded with prizes and degrees. Ordained at the age of twenty-five, he was assigned lucrative livings but generally left the running of the churches to his curates while devoting himself to scientific research and experimental farming. He kept bees and silkworms in his garden and women in his bed. His outspokenness in local *tertulias*, his musical evenings with dancing, his tangled financial affairs, the birth of yet another child with yet another woman, kept him from advancement in the church. In 1802 his elder brother died, and Hidalgo succeeded to his parish in Dolores, where he continued his style of life to the delight of his new neighbors. He made friends with Ignacio Allende, a captain in the royal army, who was a well-to-do Creole, son of Spanish parents, from San Miguel el Grande (now called San Miguel de Allende in his honor). They had similar political views. They agreed that Mexico should break away from the fraudulent monarchy of Pepe Botellas ("Joe Bottles," as Napoleon's bibulous brother on the Spanish throne was called). In Querétaro, the wife of the *Corregidor* subscribed to this view and her house became the center of a conspiracy. Similar revolutionary juntas had been established in San Miguel, Celaya, Guanajuato, San Luis Potosí and Mexico City. 1 December 1810, was the date set for the pronunciamiento. Hidalgo, the brilliant ideologue and persuasive speaker, was chosen to head the movement. In a moment of tragic pride, he accepted. The Querétaro junta sprang a leak and soon the royalist police besieged the Corregidor's house. Hearing the news in Dolores, on the eve of 16 September, Hidalgo saw that the die was cast and uttered the famous *Grito de Dolores*, the rallying cry of the Insurgency.

Followed by armed civilians, he took a banner of the Virgin of Guadalupe and made it the flag of the movement. His campaign was brief: seven months of politics and fighting, followed by four months in prison, standing trial, and waiting for his death sentence to be carried out. He was executed in Chihuahua on 30 July 1811.

The Silver Conquest of the North: Zacatecas, Aguascalientes, Durango, San Luis Potosí.

Each of these states grew around a city of the same name which is now its capital. They all owe their existence directly or indirectly to Zacatecas, for the silver strikes of 1548 that overnight turned Zacatecas into the second city of New Spain and also made it the mother-city of the north. Made bold by the Zacatecas bonanza, the entire floating population of New Spain rushed toward the inhospitable mountains of the Gran Chichimeca. Some prospectors found silver closer to Mexico City, in places like Pachuca, Real del Monte and Guanajuato. The traders and the farmers followed, creating new towns among the most successful of which was Aguascalientes, which became a separate state in 1857, and continues to derive great prosperity from agriculture.

Two key figures stand out in the foundation of Zacatecas, Juan de Tolosa and Diego de Ibarra. Tolosa was married to the most aristocratic Mestiza in New Spain, doña Leonor Cortés Moctezuma, daughter of the Conquistador and granddaughter of the Aztec Emperor. Like most of the conquistadors, he had heard about silver mines in the north. Following a friendly and informative Indian guide, he was the first to find silver-bearing rocks in a wild spot below a hill with a sinister rocky excrescence on the top which he named *la Bufa* ("pig's bladder" in Basque). Only Diego de Ibarra believed in his discovery and followed him. Ibarra, like Tolosa, had high connections in New Spain, he married the daughter of the future Viceroy, Luis de Velasco, and placed his young nephew, Francisco de Ibarra, in the Viceroy's court. The Zacatecas silver strike showed the advisability of further exploration to the north. The Viceroy commissioned the young Ibarra boy to undertake the task. Francisco de Ibarra went to Zacatecas and, with his rich uncle's backing, organized an expeditionary force for the purpose and set off in 1554. He was sixteen years old at the time.

Endowed with the touch of a modest Midas, Francisco found silver wherever he went. In what is now the State of Durango, he founded the city of that name as well as many other towns still in existence, though none of comparable importance. Crossing the highest passes of the Sierra Madre, Ibarra and his men were caught in a violent snowstorm. One of their horses froze stiff. Two weeks later, on their way back, they found it still standing, an ice statue of itself. His explorations in Chihuahua, Sonora and Sinaloa intruded on territory that presumably belonged to the north-western Reino de Nueva Galicia. Ibarra laid claim to it, and in 1562 was appointed Governor and Captain General of this vast though ill-defined domain that he named New Vizcaya. Ibarra spent the last years of his life in Sinaloa, where he died a poor man at the age of thirty-eight, after having made many men rich, and leaving a fresh-scented reputation of honest dealing with Spaniards and Indians alike.

San Luis Potosí remained throughout most of the sixteenth century a vast wilderness in the north-eastern portion of the Gran Chichimeca. It was the terrain of the indomitable Guachichiles, who held out against every assault for over forty years. Cortés, for political reasons of his own, had made a brief sortie into the area from the direction of the Gulf, where he founded Pánuco shortly after the fall of Tenochtitlán. Though he left 130 Spaniards there, each with an encomienda, and several hundred Indian allies, the town languished in the noxious climate of the Huasteca, as these lowlands are called.

After the Zacatecas boom, however, Spaniards determined to conquer the land. That was the beginning of the Chichimec war which lasted from 1552 to 1591. The Guachichiles' guerilla tactics, so swift and unexpected and, above all, so different from the ceremonial warring of the Aztecs, made them invulnerable to the Spanish soldiery. They struck suddenly, and as suddenly disappeared into the mountains, leaving trails in every direction. The Spanish forces could make no headway against them. The war did not end until military tactics were replaced by palavering and gift offerings. The men chiefly responsible for this break were a Spanish-born Franciscan from Zacatecas, Fray Diego de la Magdalena, and a Mestizo captain, Miguel Caldera.

Fray Diego, a man who took both Christ and Saint Francis at their word, approached the Guachichil-Chichimecs with exemplary courage and sweetness. In 1583, he succeeded in persuading a group of them to cease their nomadic life and start learning the arts necessary to a settled existence. Four years later, Captain Caldera, comparing Fray Diego's success with the failure of armed conflict, prevailed upon the Viceroy, Luis de Velasco II, to support him in the innovative strategy of winning a war by peaceful means. Caldera was the son of a Spanish miner and a Guachichil woman, so he could literally talk to the Indians in their own language, and prove by his mere presence among them the possibility of peaceful co-existence with the Spaniards. Peace was finally achieved when Fray Diego and Captain Caldera convinced the Guachichiles that no tribute would be expected of them, only respect for the Spanish religious and civil foundations.

Shortly after the peace was concluded, the first lodes were discovered and prospectors and traders swarmed to the new province. Though these states are relatively poor in pre-Hispanic remains, they are rich in Baroque splendors. Many books have been written on the architectural distinction of these cities, yet none of them can prepare the visitor for the impact their monuments produce. The crafts have not been forgotten and the tradition is maintained. The silver from the mines has paid for the gold of the altarpieces and the flowering stone of the doorways and facades.

Still, if it is true that words outlast marble, gold and bronze, then the poetry of a single Zacatecano, Ramón López Velarde, may well outlast all the palaces and churches of the region. He lived intensely and died young (1888-1921). His *oeuvre* is small, but one of his poems, *Suave Patria*, a celebration of Mexico's provincial life has become the national epic. Yet its scale is intimate and its images belong to our common childhood. *Suave Patria* is a recreation of provincial Mexico in the early years of this century, a scene observed through a child's eye and preserved in a child's memory. (Diego Rivera's mural of a childhood holiday in the Alameda, now in the lobby of the Prado Hotel across the street from the Alameda, could serve as an illustration for *Suave Patria*.) After school hours, the child buys sweets and toy balloons, drinks a glass of *chía* water, all the while thinking of his geography and history lessons, of Cortés and Cuauhtémoc and, reflecting on the Mexican sky, describes it as the smooth planing of herons and "the green lightening of the parrot's flight." He knows that the God-Child deeded us a stable and that our oil comes from the devil.

López Velarde himself never saw his poem in print. He wrote it to celebrate the first centennial of Mexico's independence. That year he died.

Cultura de Occidente: Michoacán, Colima, Jalisco, Nayarit

Michoacán (Náhuatl, *michihuacán*, "place of fishermen" from *michin*, fish, the possessive *hua* and the place ending *can*.)

The pre-Hispanic Tarascos were probably the only Mesoamerican people who came up from the south. Their language, metallurgy and hillside terrace farming, as well as their pit-and-chamber burial vaults, clearly link them to some of the early cultures in Peru. Though repeatedly invaded by Teotihuacanos, Toltecs and Aztecs, they managed to preserve their cultural and political autonomy.

Though their kingdom bears the Náhuatl name of Michoacán, all other place names surviving from pre-Hispanic times remained stubbornly Purépecha. (The

Tarascos, incidentally, called themselves "Purépechas." Tarscue, i.e. Tarasco, is what they called the Spaniards. It means son-in-law in Purépecha, for they too had given their nubile daughters to the conquerors, and in the general linguistic muddle the Spaniards took it to mean the name of their race.) Indeed, from the linguistic tracks they left, we know that they had settlements as far north as the Zuñi pueblos and east through most of Guanajuato and Querétaro. Avándaro ("house of rabbits") Acámbaro ("place of magueys"), Yuririapúndaro ("lake of blood") are the kind of unmistakeable signposts they left wherever they went.

Their cosmogony and religion had many similarities with that of the Aztecs, but again they managed to keep their own names for the deities and the concepts they borrowed from their powerful neighbors. Thus Pátzcuaro ("place of darkness") corresponds to the Aztecs' Paradise of the Drowned, Tlalocan (literally "place of Tlaloc" – the rain god). They called their king *Uandácuri*, "he who speaks," exactly the meaning of the Aztec *Tlatoani*, and for that matter, the Roman *dictator*. A similar coincidence is that both Tarascos and Aztecs had a deity of filth and excrement, Xaránga and Tlazoltéotl respectively, whose names exactly correspond to the Romans' Cloacina, deity of the sewers (*cloacas*).

Vasco de Quiroga (1470-1565)

The Mexican West was abysmally unlucky in its conquistadors and correspondingly fortunate in its missionaries.

The Tarascos' behavior during the Conquest can hardly be faulted. They defended their neutrality with as much verve as their independence. Their King Zuanga, who had once repelled an attack by Moctezuma II, refused the Aztecs help against the Spaniards. After Zuanga's death, twelve Aztec nobles approached his son, King Tangaxoan, with the same request. The Tarascos sacrificed them so that they could take their message personally to the dead king. Despite such adamantine attitudes, Cortés had no trouble in making friends with them. King Tangaxoan traveled to Coyoacán to meet Cortés and swear fealty to the Spanish emperor. Tangaxoan, baptized with the name of don Pedro, in 1524 invited the Franciscans to send missionaries to Michoacán.

So matters stood when Nuño de Guzmán was called from the governorship of Pánuco to form part of the First Audiencia of New Spain (1527-30). Although traditionally credited with the conquest of the west and the creation of the Reign of New Galicia, what he actually did was to slaughter the native population and leave a trail of bloodshed and terror wherever he went. Denounced to the Crown by Bishop Zumárraga, he left Mexico City, presumably to go in search of the City of the Amazons, of which he had heard exciting reports. Arriving in Michoacán, he demanded tribute from the converted king, don Pedro de Tangaxoan. Unsatisfied with the amount, he hanged this friend of Cortés and vassal of Charles V. In Jalisco he burned over 800 Indian pueblos and had their caciques *aperreados* (hounded), a process which consisted of chaining them naked together and having them torn apart by hunting dogs. He branded the natives he captured and sold them to his followers at a peso a head.

The First Audiencia had been suspended and arraigned in his absence. Cortés returned from Madrid followed by the Second Audiencia in January 1531. A posse was sent to bring Nuño de Guzmán back to Mexico City to face charges, but by the time they found him, Guzmán had already received his royal appointment as Governor of New Galicia. He took the envoys prisoner, and from that time on made it a point to defy the Second Audiencia of New Spain. Finally, in 1536, he decided to present his case personally before the King. He had the misfortune to arrive in

Mexico at the same time as the official who had been appointed to hear his case and replace him as governor of New Galicia. They met at the door of the Viceroy's apartments, and the new governor took Guzmán prisoner then and there. He was sent back to Spain, where he stood trial, received his sentence and spent the rest of his life in jail.

The Second Audiencia had all the virtues that the first one lacked. With it came Vasco de Quiroga, perhaps the only man capable of counteracting the evil done by Nuño de Guzmán in the western territories. He spent 1533 and 1534 assessing the damage done in Michoacán. The enraged and now bitterly rebellious Tarascos would not come down from the hills to which they had fled after their experience with Guzmán. Seeing the hatred and mistrust Guzmán had planted in these steadfast spirits, Vasco de Quiroga understood that the winning back of their trust was destined to be his life's work.

It was uphill all the way. Quiroga was already sixty years old, an age when most Crown officials were already maneuvering for a comfortable retirement, and he was setting himself a task more formidable perhaps than any faced by the first missionaries. The diocese of Michoacán was created in 1536 and Vasco de Quiroga was elected Bishop. There was an obstacle: he was not even a priest. So in 1538 he was ordained and consecrated Bishop on the same day – perhaps a first and only case in modern ecclesiastical history.

The corner-stone of his missionary work was to be the "*hospital-pueblo*": the infirmary and hostelry for Indian pilgrims and travelers, the municipal offices, and the quarters for the groups of married volunteers who did the nursing and housekeeping. Quiroga decreed that every church should have a hospital and a school. At his death in 1565, he left ninety-two hospitals in his diocese.

After his death, the Jesuits took over his schools, including the one where young Hidalgo had picked up all his odd ideas while the Augustinians elaborated on his primitive institutions by gathering whole native villages around their convents, which became teaching centers where new farming practices were tried out, European crops and fruit trees planted, and where the natives could practice their traditional crafts and learn new ones. As a result of Vasco's and the friars' early teachings, Michoacán now has one of the richest and most varied traditions in handicrafts. Paracho continues to make guitars, Uruapan lacquer work, Pátzcuaro feather decorations, Santa Clara copper ware, and Tzintzuntzan a magical green-glaze ceramic transcending Rococo.

The original Tarascos came down from the hills long before his death. They called him "Daddy" – "Tata" Vasco – and their descendants continue to call him so to this day.

Colima (Náhuatl, *Colliman*, "place of Colli," the aged hunchback god, bearer of fire, a reference to the nearby Volcan del Fuego). Capital, Colima.

Tenochtitlán conquered, Cortés sent his captains towards every point of the compass to explore and take possession of the land. The west fell to the lot of Cristóbal de Olid, whose peaceful takeover of the Tarascan kingdom in 1522 was so successful. King Colliman, on the other hand, proved unexpectedly tough. It took a second expedition, strengthened by several thousand Tarascos, to defeat him and to found, in 1523, the village of Colima, the first municipality in New Spain. Finding the climate unbearable, the leader of the expedition returned to Mexico City. Colima was a hardship post no one wanted.

It was in danger of reverting to nature, or to the natives, when Cortés remembered a young relation of his, Francisco Cortés de Buenaventura, and offered him the post, adding as an inducement the story of the City of the Amazons – "where no men ever were" – and a commission to seek it out and conquer it. Young Cortés could not contain his enthusiasm and soon set out on a new expedition. The youthful troops followed their captain, hacking their way enthusiastically through the underbrush, wading streams and skirting swamps, sustained by their romantic vision. They went as far north as Tepic before discouragement set in. The closest they came to finding a city of Amazons was in the nearby town of Xalixco, which was ruled by a woman (as in fact the State of Colima is now – by Griselda Alvarez, an extraordinary poet, teacher, and the first woman governor in Mexico).

On their return journey, young Cortés and his men were met by apparitions. In a valley near a beautiful bay, the dense underbrush suddenly blossomed into a myriad of colored flags, and Indians jumped out, disposed to fight. Though startled at first, the Spaniards shot a volley into the tree-tops. The natives at once proved amenable to reason, and a truce was reached. The spot is still called the Valley of Flags (Valle de Banderas) in memory of the occasion and gave its name to the nearby Bahía de Banderas, site of the lyrically lovely ex-village of Puerto Vallarta.

Back in Colima, the Spaniards moved the original town from the torrid lowlands to the pleasant valley under the volcano where it now stands. (Until March 1982 it was the only active volcano in Mexico. At this writing, however, a volcano in Chiapas, the Chichonal, has resumed its activity, burying in a series of eruptions the surrounding towns under a layer of ashes.) This snow-capped cone rising above the mango and coconut groves of Colima dominates everything around it, the feathery, dark ravines, the intensely cultivated fields, even the glint of the faraway sea and the daily extravaganza put on by the setting sun. When the volcano begins to mumble, it rivets everyone's attention. It blows smoke-rings into the morning sky and puts on a show-stopping molten-lava act that is particularly impressive at night. But when it shakes the earth around it, its splendor is forgotten, and terrified parents with bundled up children rush out of their houses in the middle of the night, while somewhere nearby, another Classic burial vault may crack open, disgorging its disorganized bones with their company of dancing Xólotl dogs, celestial warriors, all looking bewildered under the open sky.

Jalisco (Náhuatl, *xalixco*, "on a sandy plain," from *xalli*, sand, *ixtli*, surface, and locative ending – *co*). Capital: Guadalajara (Arabic, *Wadi-al-hajara*, "river of pebbles.")

Nayarit (Name of the founder of the kingdom of the Cora Indians.) Capital: Tepic.

New Galicia was Nuño de Guzmán's brainchild, offspring of his megalomania and his gnawing envy of Cortés. At its height it comprised part of Zacatecas, Aguascalientes, San Luis Potosí, Durango and Sinaloa, and all of Jalisco and Nayarit. After receiving the charter of New Galicia and his appointment as governor, Nuño founded his capital in Tepic, which he called Compostela, in 1532. After his death, one of his successors moved Compostela to a valley south of Tepic in 1540. The following year the Indians rose up in arms against the Spaniards throughout New Galicia, from the northernmost settlement of Culiacán, in Sinaloa, to Guadalajara. Such Indian revolts led in 1548 to the creation of the Audiencia of New Galicia, subject to the Audiencia of New Spain in Mexico City. The members of this Audiencia were a vicious lot. Though they had neither the power nor the autonomy enjoyed by Nuño de Guzmán and the First Audiencia of New Spain, they were far enough from Mexico City to do a great deal of damage before they were suspended and arraigned in 1558. The capital of New Galicia, the Audiencia, and the diocese, were then moved from Compostela to Guadalajara in 1560, a date which marks the effective beginning of Guadalajara's subsequent power, and Jalisco's overwhelming importance in western Mexico.

Guadalajara, despite its early foundation in 1532, had inauspicious and precarious beginnings. It was founded first here, then moved there, then somewhere else, like a chess piece in Guzmán's New Galicia power game against New Spain, until it finally settled down in 1540 and grew roots in its present site. It was still a very small town in 1700, with a population of roughly 500 Creoles, 500 Negro and mulatto slaves, and 500 Mestizos. By that time, however, the surrounding mines had been pouring their bullion for a long time into Guadalajara's coffers, and the wealth was beginning to show in the solid government buildings and the convents scattered about – all built in the golden quarry stone that gives Guadalajara's architecture its distinctive late afternoon glow.

The Cora War

The unsubdued Indians of Nayarit seriously hampered commerce. They attacked haciendas, trade routes, and the rich mine of Espíritu Santo near Compostela. They were obviously arming themselves and preparing to do battle. They repulsed the advances of the missionaries. Their remoteness from Guadalajara and the Audiencia gave the Coras and the Huicholes ample time to organize themselves. The Coras were especially warlike. Their kingdom in the mountains was founded by Nayarit, a warrior and lawgiver who reigned at the time of the Conquest, and the nation he founded resisted Spanish authority until well into the eighteenth century. After a long and unremitting campaign, the Coras were starved out of their towns and finally abandoned their sanctuaries in the highest mountains. The government soldiers looted their houses and found, in the principal sanctuary, the Coras' most sacred relic: the skeleton of Nayarit, which was sent, together with the ritual vestments and vessels, to the Viceroy. An *auto da fé* was celebrated in Mexico City in which Nayarit's skeleton was solemnly burned at the stake to symbolize the end of the war and the defeat of the Coras.

The truth of the matter is that, though defeated, neither the Coras nor the more peaceable Huicholes have ever surrendered. They co-exist, but in no way mix, with the rest of the population. They continue to practice their animist religion, to paint the same stripes on their faces and celebrate the traditional festivals. They recognize no territorial boundaries other than those of their ancestral lands. Their pilgrimage routes cut across modern state lines and the obstacles of modern industrial civilization. Rails, roads and cars mean no more to them than additional new hazards in their wilderness. They still trek every year over the sierras to the Valley of the Moon, in San Luis Potosí, in order to collect the tender buttons of the new peyote, the Eucharist of their religion. This is of central importance in their lives. Everything, including crops and children, depends on the observance of these rites. It is interesting to note that the ultimately unsuccessful meetings between the Cora chieftains and the Viceroy's envoy occurred in Peyotlán – the place of the peyote.

San Blas and Guadalajara

Jalisco resisted the amputation of the large and profitable province of Tepic, and continued to demand its re-incorporation until Nayarit finally achieved statehood in 1917. Its mines and haciendas had provided substantial revenues for the state, and the loss of San Blas left Jalisco, despite its extensive shoreline, without a port on the Pacific.

San Blas had converted Guadalajara from a modest provincial capital at the start of the Insurgency in 1810 into the second city of the republic. After the transfer of the

Audiencia and see from Compostela to Guadalajara, probably no event had a greater influence on this city than the construction of the port at San Blas. As early as 1767, that corporate trouble-shooter and efficiency expert of the Bourbon kings of Spain, José de Gálvez, had decided two things: that New Spain should be divided into Intendancies, and that a northern naval base and shipyards were indispensable and should be established in the bay of San Blas. Apart from his own brilliance and achievements, Gálvez had the best family credentials. His elder brother Matías rose from a peasant origin to become the forty-eighth Viceroy of New Spain. His nephew Bernardo, who had been an excellent governor of Louisiana in the early 1780's (Galveston, Texas, was named in his honor), became the forty-ninth Viceroy of New Spain – and his equestrian portrait in Chapultepec, a suave academically-painted figure astride a wildly calligraphic steed, is one of the marvels of colonial painting.

The King himself supported José de Gálvez's plans, yet vested interests were opposed to both the Intendancies and the port. The port was eventually built, however, and in 1768 the first small fleet sailed out of San Blas toward the Californias, carrying a detachment of troops and some Jesuit missionaries. In 1788, two frigates sailed north and did not turn back until they had established contact with the Russian fur traders in Alaska. But it was the Mexican War of Independence that shifted San Blas into sudden prominence and Guadalajara to wealth and power.

The first wave of the Insurgency fizzled out in New Galicia. The Nayarit insurgents were routed, and the royalist troops cleared the road between Guadalajara and San Blas. As the war cut New Galicia off from its markets and sources of supply – central Mexico was a battlefield and Veracruz lived under permanent siege –, San Blas became the port of entry for all foreign goods, and Guadalajara became the distribution center for north-western Mexico.

The trade route that developed between San Blas and Guadalajara laid the foundations for the latter's prosperity. Guadalajara teemed with new arrivals from every walk of life. Peasants and hacendados flocked to the city for safety, taking their valuables with them. Tradesmen and professional men found a brisk demand for their talents. In the first few years of the war, the population increased from thirty to forty thousand.

This sudden affluence showed in the face of the city. A building boom followed after the war, gathering in a sumptuous architectural effect the widely scattered monuments of its Baroque and Neo-Classical past. Garden squares framed churches, and blocks of arcades framed the squares. And throughout the city, the same golden quarry stone that built the earliest convents and palaces continued to provide the *basso continuo* for the noble urban harmonies of Guadalajara

116. *Guanajuato (Guanajuato). Panoramic view, with the Basílica de Nuestra Señora on Plaza de la Paz at the center. In colonial times Guanajuato was a great center for silver mining, from which it derived its wealth.*

117. *Tula (Hidalgo). The famous carved stone figures known as the Atlantes of Tula. They stand on the top of the Temple of the Morning Star, and originally supported the roof of the temple. Tula was the ancient Toltec capital, founded at the beginning of the tenth century AD and destroyed by fire about 1165, during a Chichimec invasion.*

118. *Teotihuacán (Mexico). The Causeway of the Dead, in the ceremonial center. Though the Teotihuacán culture spanned most of the first millenium after Christ, the Sacred City itself, conceived on a colossal scale, was sacked and put to the torch sometime in the seventh or eighth centuries.*

119. *Tula (Hidalgo). An Atlante. There are four of these giant stone figures: they are not monoliths, being made up of four pieces each, and were brought back to their original position on the upper platform after being discovered in the center of the pyramid.*

120. *Malinalco (Mexico). The Temple compound. The central structure is entirely hewn out of the rock. (Aztec culture, 1325-1521).*

121. *Teotihuacán (Mexico). The Pyramid of the Moon. With the Pyramid of the Sun, this is the most imposing edifice in Teotihuacán and, given its dominating position at one end of the Causeway of the Dead, may have been the more important of the two, suggesting that a matriarchal society preceded the patriarchal religion of the sun worshipers.*

124

125

122. *Guanajuato, the church of La Valenciana, Mexican High Baroque, built between 1765 and 1788. The Valenciana mine came to produce two-thirds of Mexico's silver in the eighteenth century, when Mexico itself was producing two-thirds of the world's silver.*

123. *A typical church facade of the heartland region.*

124. *Near Apon (Hidalgo). The fortified gate of the* pulque *hacienda of Tetlapaya.*

125. *San Miguel de Allende (Guanajuato). A row of houses in this attractive colonial town, which has been classified as a national monument and has thus been able to preserve much of its original character.*

126

126. *Guadalajara (Jalisco). The cathedral, built between 1558 and 1616 and continually modified to the present day, stands at the center of a monumental Latin cross formed by the four open squares around it.*

127. *A church in Guadalajara.*

127

128

129

128. *Morelia (Michoacán). The main courtyard of the Palacio Clavijiero.*

129. *Guadalajara (Jalisco). The Hospicio Cabañas. An orphanage founded by Bishop Ruiz de Cabañas in 1801 and endowed with the rent of one city house for each orphan.*

130. *On the road from Pachuca to Ciudad Sahagún (Hidalgo). "The arches of Fray Tembleque." This greatest of Mexican aqueducts was built in the sixteenth century by a Franciscan friar with no previous experience of building. The double arch spanning a gorge at the center rises to a greater height than the Roman aqueduct at Segovia in Spain.*

131

131. La Quemada (Zacatecas). One of the most important archeological sites in the north of Mexico. The ancient name of this ruined city is not known for certain, but it has been tentatively identified as Chicomóztoc, which means "Seven caves." Legend has it that the seven Nahua tribes lived here for nine years before they separated.

132. Real de Catorce (San Luis Potosí). El Palenque – the cock-fighting arena. The old mining town of Real de Catorce is in the neighborhood of the ceremonial valleys of the peyote culture.

133 La Valenciana (Guanajuato). The main staircase outside the church.

134. Querétaro (capital of Querétaro). Decorative column on the side of a building.

132

33

134

135

135. A charreada (or Mexican rodeo) today. The charro *is the man responsible for the* hacienda's *wealth. At his best he represents the backbone of the country. Reliable, genial, hospitable and hardworking, he lives in constant touch with the land, the animals and the plants that feed him.*

136. A bull in the corral, with a charro *hat typical of northern Mexico in the foreground.*

137. A turn of the century painting of a charreada, *the original rodeo, by Icaza, a Mexican painter of the* charro *genre. The* charro, *or Mexican cowboy, was largely responsible for the settling of the cattle country of northern Mexico, Texas and the American south-west.*

136

137

138. Courtyard of a working hacienda *today. The* haciendas *were the unit of rural survival during the seventeenth century. Every* hacienda *became self-sufficient producing everything necessary to feed and clothe its own people. A few of the* haciendas *have survived intact from the sixteenth and seventeenth centuries to the present day.*

139. Charro *hats in a room in a* hacienda.

140

140. *Actopan (Hidalgo). Sixteenth-century frescoes in the stairwell of the Augustinian monastery, now transformed into a colonial museum.*

141

142

141. *Actopan (Hidalgo). The Bóveda de Actopan, a vast "open chapel" containing murals, covered by a magnificent vault (bóveda) with a span of nearly 56 feet.*

142. *Guadalajara (Jalisco). Interior of the Hospicio Cabañas. The murals in the chapel of this orphanage were painted by José Clemente Orozco in 1939, and are generally considered his masterpiece.*

143. *Santa Mónica (Zacatecas). Grain silos on a hacienda. The conical silo form dates from pre-Hispanic times.*

Chapter 5
The Frontier States

The States of Baja California and Baja California Sur, Coahuila, Chihuahua, Nuevo León, Tamaulipas, Sonora, Sinaloa.

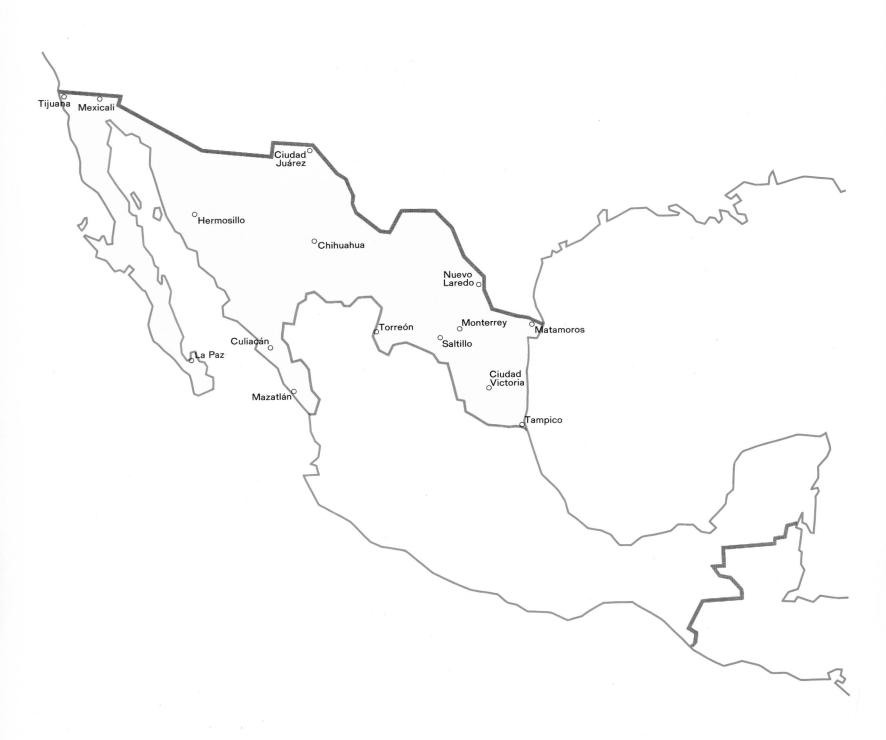

The biggest and richest of Mexico's border states is Texas. The next biggest and richest is California. Unfortunately for Mexico, they are both now on the American side of the border and have been for over a hundred years. The time element is unimportant, though, and many Mexicans continue to experience flashing pains as a result of the amputation. This sad story must be told once again if our frontier history is to make any sense.

Spain had won and settled that land, Mexico had given it independence and freed the soil from slavery. Yet Mexico must take its share of blame for the loss if the enormity of the subsequent American injustice is to be seen in fair perspective. The Mexican Republic came out of its War of Independence totally depleted, and lacking both the human and the economic resources to maintain its enormous and empty northern territories. But instead of retrenching and reorganizing, it annexed an additional 180,000 square miles of the Central American provinces. Such over-extension made the new republic vulnerable on every side.

Since the story can most concisely be told in chronological order, we should start at the very beginning, with Charles Martel turning back the tide of Islam at Poitiers in 732 AD. The Moslems settled down in the Iberian peninsula and legend had it that a Portuguese bishop, unwilling to accept the new overlords, sailed west with his retainers and there, in some distant islands, founded the Seven Cities of Cíbola.

In the tales of medieval chivalry, these cities had floors of gold and walls of cut crystal. Cortés and many of the conquistadors knew these knightly legends well. He even named the Californias after the mythic land mentioned as Californe in the *Chanson de Roland* and as California in *The Exploits of Esplandian (Las Sergas de Esplandián)*, a sequel to *Amadis de Gaule*, published in Seville in 1510. So when the conquistadors heard the Náhuatl-speaking natives saying they came from the north, from the venerated Seven Caves, they put seven and seven together and came up with a confusion of wishful thinking. The search for the Golden Cities of Cíbola, or Quívira, was the motive behind the earliest northern explorations. The story goes on like this.

1536 Alvar Núñez Cabeza de Vaca, shipwrecked in 1528 off the coast of Texas, arrived in Sinaloa after an eight-year trek across the continent. He brought back a vivid account of his wanderings over what is now most of the border territory, which he later wrote up as *Los Naufragios (The Shipwrecks)*, complete with charts and precise geographical descriptions. He also brought hearsay reports of the golden cities, which led to the expedition of Francisco Vázquez de Coronado, one of the few financed directly by the Spanish Crown. Coronado followed up the rumors and found nothing but straggles of adobe huts and the cliffside dwellings of the Pueblo Indians. His expedition made important discoveries, however, among them the Grand Canyon.

1581 Later expeditions explored the area that cartographers began to designate as New Mexico.

1605 The foundation of Santa Fe, the second oldest city of the U.S., after Saint Augustine in Florida.

1686 The Governor of Nuevo Reino de León issued orders from Monterrey for the exploration and settlement of Texas with people from Saltillo, San Esteban de la Nueva Tlaxcala, and Monclova in the neighboring province of Coahuila. The colonization of Texas was carried out in the Roman style of civic and military outposts — in this case missions and presidios — rather than in the Anglo-Saxon fashion of homesteaders devoted to cultivating the land.

1717 The French assaults on the north-eastern border of New Spain provoked the Spanish authorities to more intensive settlement. Six missions were founded in

1716 and 1717, and San Antonio and El Alamo in the following year. Many were destroyed in the ensuing conflict; in 1721, the presidio of San Antonio de Béjar was founded and became the modern city of San Antonio.

1727 The Texas territory was established, though only its western border with Louisiana was defined.

1803 The Louisiana Purchase brought in an aggressive, expansionist American population. Three abortive American invasions were repelled.

1819 The Onís-Adams (Florida) Treaty between the U.S. and Spain defined the boundary lines. The U.S. relinquished all claims on Texas contingent on the Louisiana Purchase. The Treaty was already academic, since by 1819 Spain had been routed from most of Mexico's territory.

1821 The newly independent Mexico granted Moses Austin license to establish a foreign colony in Texas. Many southerners arrived with their slaves, in violation of Mexican law.

1824 Mexico's first Federal Constitution created the state of Coahuila-Texas.

1826 The American Minister to Mexico, Joel Pointsett, offered to buy the eastern half of Texas for 1 million dollars. Mexico refused.

1829 Anthony Butler replaced Pointsett, with instructions to insist on the purchase of Texas.

1830 Mexico woke up to the danger of unchecked immigration, and prohibited further immigration. By this time there were four Americans to every Mexican in Texas.

1833 American settlers in San Antonio rejected the authority of the Coahuila-Texas government, and applied to the Mexican Congress for separate statehood.

1835 Santa Anna's centralist constitution, which had swept away states rights, reinforced the secessionist movement that had been building up among the Texas Americans. Austin had rejected secession in favor of an alliance with the liberal-federalist party in Mexico. The secessionists set up a provisional government to fight for their independence. Sam Houston began hostilities against the virtually defenseless presidios which Mexico had long neglected. The patent weakness of the Mexican liberal-federalist party convinced even the anti-secessionists of the need to become independent. American homesteaders in Texas sought U.S. support.

1836 6 March - 21 April. Santa Anna beseiged and massacred the men entrenched in the Alamo. Yelling "Remember the Alamo!" Sam Houston defeated Santa Anna in San Jacinto, took him prisoner, and brought the war to an end.

1837 The Lone Star Republic was recognized by the U.S., Great Britain and France.

Up to this point, Mexico must bear the blame for losing Texas. What happened next, though, will remain forever a blot on the history of the United States. California had been attracting more and more American immigrants. An important political group in Washington set its sights on the acquisition of California.

1843 Charles Frémont's expedition to California. His report described the boundless economic potential of the region and the flimsiness of Mexican defenses.

1845 The Lone Star Republic was admitted to the Union. Mexico broke diplomatic relations with the U.S. over the annexation of one of its rebellious provinces.
June – The U.S. Secretary of the Navy ordered Commodore Sloat to seize San Francisco as soon as the war with Mexico was declared.
July – President James Polk sent an army detachment under General Zachary Taylor to the Nueces River, the southern-most boundary of Texas since its creation as a province of New Spain.

November – Polk sent Minister Plenipotentiary John Slidell to Mexico with a set of proposals, including the extension of Texas south to the Río Grande, the purchase for 5 million dollars of New Mexico, which then included Arizona, and a "money-is-no-object" proposal for the purchase of California. Mexico did not receive Slidell.

1846 13 January – Polk ordered General Taylor to cross the Nueces River and occupy the northern bank of the Río Grande.

25 April – Mexican cavalry crossed the Río Grande, killing some American soldiers and capturing the rest in the skirmish that followed.

11 May – President Polk urged Congress to declare war against Mexico in the following terms: "The cup of forbearance has been exhausted. After reiterated menaces, Mexico has passed the boundary of the United States, has invaded our territory and shed American blood upon American soil." Two days later, Congress declared war.

Outraged by the war, Henry David Thoreau refused to pay his taxes and went to jail for it. Later, back in Walden, he wrote his *Essay on Civil Disobedience*, to justify his actions. The work continues to be the handbook of every man protesting against illegal regimes and unjust wars.

1847 22 December – A freshman Whig representative from Illinois by the name of Abraham Lincoln demanded that Polk reveal the exact spot on American soil where American blood had been shed.

1848 12 January – Receiving no answer from Polk, Lincoln again took the floor, accused Polk of provoking the war and characterized his efforts to put the blame on Mexico as "the half-insane mumblings of a fever-dream."

"The record is clear," wrote Morrison, Commager and Leuchenburg in *A Concise History of the American Republic*. "Polk baited Mexico into war over the Texas boundary in order to get California."

1853 Postscript

The 1849 gold rush turned San Francisco into the emporium of the west. The railroads followed the rush. The Pacific Railroad needed the strip of Mexican land south of the Gila River known as the Mesilla of Arizona. Prospectors, Indians, and squatters swarmed in, and once more Mexico and the United States seemed set on a collision course. Presidents Pierce and Santa Anna preferred to negotiate. The result was the Gadsden Purchase – or Mesilla Treaty – which gave the U.S. an additional 110,000 square kilometers for 10 million dollars, 7 million to be paid on signing, the rest after agreement on the southern boundary.

July – The Mexican Consul in New York showed up to receive the first payment, though he had no legal power to do so. The Mexican Foreign Office ordered its Consul in New Orleans post haste to New York to retrieve the money. The New York Consul gave him only 6.8 million, the difference having gone to make "certain payments." Following his example, the New Orleans Consul pocketed sixty-eight thousand as his commission. Summarily fired by Santa Anna, he published a defense of his action to the effect that being a civil servant did not make him the government's slave, and that in view of his bad health and the arduousness of the journey undertaken, his 1% commission was quite moderate, the usual commission being 2%.

The only wonder is that, with such officials, we did not lose the rest of the country in those giddy first years of Independence.

"After great pain, a sudden stillness comes." If Mexico's long northern wound has by now become a scar, it continues to produce irritation on both sides of the border. And the border itself remains the permanent joint headache of the Mexican and the American governments. There is a brisk illicit traffic of American goods into Mexico and of Mexican bodies into the U.S. It has been called the widest two-way street in the world.

The Revolution

The Mexican north is still in many ways a barbarous territory. It lacks the cultural unity that a dense population and a rich colonial culture gave the rest of the country as far north as the Zacatecas silver routes. The Conquest and settlement of the northern states constituted the last, painfully prolonged stage of the Chichimeca War. The Sonora Yaqui War, for example, signed its most recent armistice with President Cárdenas as late as 1937.

In this context, it is difficult not to see the 1910 Revolution as a sociological sequel to the ethnic conflicts of the many Chichimeca wars. The firmly established south has always been the seat of government, imposing its will on the refractory north. Don Porfirio's regime was quintessentially southern in both geographical makeup and psychological outlook. Its overthrow represented an uprising of the north against the authority of the south. With the exception of Zapata, the leaders of the Revolution were all northerners: Madero and Carranza from Coahuila, Pancho Villa from Durango and Chihuahua, Obregón and Calles from Sonora.

Francisco I. Madero was the scion of a rich Coahuila land-owning family. Though he held the economic views of his class, he rebelled against the political stranglehold of the southern hierarchy and don Porfirio's dictatorship. To his own father's amazement, this singularly gentle son succeeded in carrying out the first legitimate election in thirty years and then ousting the dictator with a minimum of bloodshed. This he accomplished in exactly six months, from 20 November 1910, when the first shots were fired in Puebla, to 25 May 1911, when don Porfirio signed his resignation in Ciudad Juárez, Chihuahua. With the dictator's removal the purpose of the Revolution was presumably accomplished. Very little Mexican blood had been shed. As it turned out, however, the Revolution had only just started, and it proceeded apace.

Revolts and counter revolts succeeded one another and could only be settled by bullets, battles and assassinations. The successful framing of the 1917 Constitution in Querétaro is a matter of sheer, blessed luck, because by that time the Revolutionary movement was shattered, and its factions at each other's throats.

The maverick Pancho Villa dominated the phase of the Revolution beginning with Madero's uprising and ending with the 1917 Constitution. Born in Durango, he became an outlaw as a youngster, after shooting his hacendado boss whom he found trying to rape his sister. The Revolution was made to order for him. He had already moved on to Chihuahua by that time, and there mounted the first rebel attacks on Ciudad Juárez and other border towns. Supported by his crack cavalry division *División del Norte*, he became governor of Chihuahua between 1913 and 1915 (a fact most Mexicans ignore). In 1914 he broke with Carranza, the Constitutionalist leader, joined forces with Zapata and went on with him to Mexico City.

As governor of Chihuahua, he effected some sound monetary reforms and kicked out the Spanish business men who had supported Huerta, Madero's assassin. He initiated his brand of agrarian reform, which he saw as the breaking up of the gigantic *latifundios* into small private landholdings. John Reed, the radical American journalist who later wrote about the Russian Revolution in *Ten Days that Shook the World*, followed Villa around for a time and in his book, *Insurgent Mexico*, recorded Villa's populist notions of an agrarian military republic, in which every citizen would divide his time equally between farm work and military service, and would thus form a standing army for the defense of the country.

After Pancho Villa's break with Carranza, "the strong men of Sonora" came to the fore, Alvaro Obregón, the great warrior, and Plutarco Elías Calles, the consummate politician. Pancho Villa's apotheosis was the taking of Mexico City with Zapata and his men. After that, Villa's luck changed. Or perhaps his marathon philandering took its toll. (He had in his personal guard a court entertainer who played the piano for him in his favorite brothels and restaurants, a fifteen-year-old lieutenant, Agustín Lara, who later became Mexico's most popular song-writer). He lost battle after battle to Obregón in the central states; his División del Norte started melting away. Pancho Villa returned to his power base in Chihuahua and attempted to invade Sonora but was ignominiously defeated by Calles in Agua Prieta. After that, he returned to his outlaw existence as a guerilla fighter in the Chihuahua mountains he knew so well. He returned to civil life after a general amnesty had been declared in 1920. An old run-down hacienda had been given to him as a reward for his revolutionary services, and there he retired with a small number of his more faithful troopers to repair the *casco*, farm the land and raise livestock. Someone must have found his presence, however quiescent, too much of a potential threat. In 1923 Pancho Villa was ambushed and shot as he was driving back to his hacienda from Parral.

The sequel to Pancho Villa's story is singularly gruesome. In 1926, three years after his death, his grave was broken open and his corpse decapitated. But like Saint Anthony of Padua in life, Pancho Villa seems to have possessed the gift of ubiquity after death. For several years after the incident, traveling "carnivals" still showed the 5,000 dollars WANTED poster of Pancho Villa along with the "authentic head of the notorious Mexican bandit," many of which were exhibited simultaneously in different towns.

The period between the Aguascalientes Convention of 1914 and the shooting of President Carranza in 1920 was perhaps the bloodiest part of the Revolution. It took the next two presidents, Obregón (1920-24) and Calles (1924-28), all their time to rein in the wildly charging forces of a nation run amok. One rebellion succeeded another, all of which were successfully quelled. The most important was the Cristero Rebellion of 1926 to 1929, which ended when the government declared a general amnesty to the rebellious priests though without changing one iota the "anti-clerical" constitutional articles that had provoked the outbreak.

In 1929, Calles, no longer President but definitely the strong man of Mexico, brought this wide-spread rebelliousness to an end with a stroke of political genius: the bringing together of all 200 warring parties under one ecumenical umbrella, the PNR (Partido Nacional Revolucionario), grandfather of the present day PRI (Partido Revolucionario Institucional), which was grandly designed to be all things to all men.

Ironically, this immensely effective institution created by a northerner became the political booty of the south practically from its inception. No northerner has since been elected president, although a couple of them have occupied the presidency in an interim status. This may seem an essentially frivolous observation until one thinks back on Mexico's history. The north carried out the Revolution and left its progressive imprint on the 1917 Constitution. The party the northerners created to represent the will and the regional interests of the entire republic has been co-opted by southerners who have formed a hereditary, oligarchic élite with a monopoly on political power that differs very little from the oligarchy expelled by the Revolution except in the magnitude of the fortunes now amassed and in the extent of official corruption.

The banner slogan of the Revolution, "Effective Suffrage, No Re-election," has been technically observed in its letter, though hardly in its spirit. A congressman is elected first for one district, then for another. A woman senator for a northern state immediately after the end of her term becomes a representative for one of the Mexico City congressional districts. The posts are kept for and rotated among the members of "the Great Revolutionary Family," as the hereditary élite is known. The crowning irony is reserved for the presidency. Though the candidate goes through the exhausting motions and the unbelievable expense of a national campaign with fleets of planes, helicopters and air-conditioned buses, and, at the end of the campaign a national election does take place, the entire proceedings are pure theater. The incumbent president picks his successor and the PRI sees to it that he gets a majority of votes. And the elective presidency paid for by more than a million lives has for the last two terms been occupied by men who have never held an elective post before as is also the case of the candidate for the 1982-88 term. So the Revolution dreamed up by the anarchists and ideologues, made and won by warriors, is now the power preserve of the bureaucrats.

El Nuevo Reino de León

The settlement of the northern provinces of Nuevo León, Coahuila and Tamaulipas, the "Second Conquest of New Spain," was carried out by later generations of conquistadors beginning in the second half of the sixteenth century and ending in the course of the eighteenth century with the settlement of Texas and the Californias and the conquest of Tamaulipas. Its history hinges on the fortunes of single cities, rather than of provinces and as such it must be told.

The city of Saltillo, now the capital of Coahuila, was at one time the capital of the slave trade. When del Canto founded it in 1577, shortly before founding Santa Lucia (Monterrey), Saltillo still belonged to Nueva Vizcaya, from whose capital of Durango del Canto's expedition had orginally started. Located in a fertile valley, it was the only one of del Canto's foundations to survive and have a continuous though not untroubled existence. Saltillo had a precarious existence until 1589, when Miguel Caldera, the remarkable Mestizo captain who put an end to the Gran Chichimec war in San Luis Potosí two years later, arrived to palaver with the local Indians. Being half Guachichil himself, he convinced the Coahuila Chichimecs of the possibility of peaceful co-existence. The Viceroy Luis de Velasco II, applying the measures that were later to be so successful in San Luis Potosí, prevailed on the chief of the Tlaxcalan Republic to allow 400 families to settle as homesteaders in the northern marches. In 1591, the rich Spanish miner, Francisco de Urdiñola, founded alongside Saltillo its Indian twin city of San Esteban de Nueva Tlaxcala and went on from there to found Concepción del Oro and the hacienda of Patos, which became the headquarters of Mexico's greatest latifundio.

Divided by the breadth of a single street, Saltillo and San Esteban were worlds apart in their judicial, religious and administrative organization. Saltillo depended judicially from the Audiencia of Guadalajara, administratively from Durango, capital of New Vizcaya, and ecclesiastically from the see of New Galicia, whereas San Esteban depended directly from the viceroy and the authority of the capital of New Spain. The Tlaxcalan settlers enjoyed privileges no other Indians had at the time. They could ride horseback, bear arms, place the honorific "don" (from *dominus*) before their names; best of all, they did not pay taxes either to the Guadalajara Audiencia or the New Vizcaya treasury. This most enviable of exemptions eventually erased the borderline between the two cities. San Esteban became a tax shelter for the Saltillo Spaniards and soon the distinction between the two cities disappeared. No discord developed between the two racial groups because their very distinct economic activities never came into competition. The Spaniards grew wheat, bred livestock and founded related industries such as flour mills, tanneries and textile mills, while the Tlaxcalans grew vegetables, fruit trees and practiced their native handicrafts. Theirs were two complementary economies that enriched and never embittered their relationship.

Saltillo's prosperity and growth were such that it soon began to provide settlers for the less fortunate neighboring towns. Monterrey, now the capital of Nuevo León, was one of its first beneficiaries. An exotic strain marks the town's beginnings. In 1579, Luis de la Cueva y Carvajal, a Portuguese of Jewish ancestry, received a charter from Philip II to explore, conquer, pacify and settle a gigantic area bounded on the west by a line extending from Pánuco (Veracruz) to the bay of Corpus Christi (then San José, in Texas) and projecting thence in a north-easterly direction for 200 leagues. The geographic specifications of the charter are so vague that no two modern versions of what the grant comprised agree with one another. The concession was so enormous, however, that whichever way it is interpreted it included most of what are now the states of Texas, Coahuila, Nuevo León and Tamaulipas.

Carvajal brought with him many New Christians (converts from Judaism) exempted from providing proof of their religious orthodoxy and the purity of their blood, a remarkable concession on Philip II's part.

In 1579 Carvajal founded San Luis Rey de Francia on the site of the future Monterrey. The following year he went on to Saltillo, showed the inhabitants his charter and recruited a sufficient number to found Almadén on the ruins of La Trinidad, whence he left to continue exploring the boundless lands of his charter. The lieutenant he left in Almadén, disappointed with the poverty of the mines, persuaded the remaining settlers to follow him north to what they began then to call New Mexico. None of their settlements survived.

The machinations of his enemies finally brought Carvajal to the tribunals of the Inquisition, accused of slave trading and being faithful to his old religion. He was arrested and taken to Mexico City, his wife and sister were also arrested, tortured and burned at the stake. He died in the dungeons of the Inquisition in 1590 of what sounds suspiciously like a broken heart.

Shortly after Carvajal's arrest, his settlement was abandoned and the Indians burned it to the ground. In 1596, the treasurer of the town, Diego de Montemayor, decided to reconstruct the settlement; calling it Monterrey in honor of the reigning viceroy. Though the town did not founder again, it did not begin to grow and prosper until 1611, when a Zacatecas silver millionaire, Augustín de Zavala, was named governor of the province.

Agustín de Zavala never went to Monterrey. He governed through agents and justices until his son Martín acquired a royal charter in Madrid and returned in 1626 to take over the management of the Nuevo Reino de León. He offered extensive grants for the settlement of Querétaro and San Miguel and shortly thereafter the first flocks of sheep arrived. Sheep raising turned out to be such a lucrative business that it soon became one of the preferred investments of the colonial nobility of New Spain. By the middle of the eighteenth century, flocks numbering millions migrated from Querétaro and Guanajuato to Nuevo León and Nuevo Santander (Tamaulipas), where they spent the winter, were sheared in the spring and herded back to their home pastures for the summer. This migratory type of sheep walk, similar to the Spanish *mesta*, though immensely profitable to the owners of the flocks, virtually destroyed the Nuevo León countryside, leaving it an overgrazed desert. The walks, however, blazed the trails for the missions, presidios and entrepots. The merchants who followed these trails specialized naturally in goods like corn fodder, hides, wool and its products, and in time established tanneries and woolen mills which were the first industries that appeared in Monterrey.

For a long time after its foundation Monterrey was so closely identified with the Nuevo Reino de León that it was referred to as "el Reino" and its natives as "reineros."

The Zavala family consolidated the prosperity of the Nuevo Reino de León and turned Monterrey into the metropolis of the far north. Martín Zavala died there in 1664 after thirty-eight years of efficient rule. Four years later, Alonso de León the Younger became governor and in 1686 undertook the first systematic exploration and settlement of Texas with troops and settlers from Nuevo León, Monclova, Saltillo, San Esteban de Nueva Tlaxcala, and many more Tlaxcalans from the town of San Juan de Tlaxcala, founded by his father, the chronicler, in 1646.

Coahuila remained a part of the Reino until 1689, when Alonso de León, returning from his Texas expedition, ordered the resettlement of Almadén, which had become a ghost town, and called the new city Santiago de Monclova, upon which Coahuila became a separate province with Monclova as its capital. Monclova, incidentally, was named in honor of the reigning Viceroy, the Count of Monclova, nicknamed "the Silver-Armed" not because of his weapons, his wealth or his strength in battle, but because he had lost an arm in battle and had an artificial arm made entirely of silver plate.

Monclova, on the site of the pre-Hispanic Cuauhuilan, remained the capital of the province until 1824, when the first federal constitution of the Mexican republic made Saltillo the capital of Coahuila-Texas.

Tamaulipas

Nuevo León, Coahuila and Texas moved into the eighteenth century under the aegis of Monterrey, which during the previous century had outstripped every other northern city. Of all the provinces included in Carvajal's royal charter, only Tamaulipas stagnated. It was then still known as the Province of Pánuco, after the city founded by Cortés in 1522 on the Pánuco River, Tamaulipas's southern boundary. Many later missions and settlements failed. Pánuco itself barely survived. The plaguey swamps, the heat, the insects, the epidemics drove all the would-be settlers out.

During his tenure of office in Pánuco, the unspeakable Nuño de Guzmán, true to type, did as much harm as anybody could in such a short time. Finding neither deposits of precious metals nor large settlements of sedentary Indians willing to work for the conquistadors' comfort and enrichment, his enlightened self-interest showed him the next best thing to do and he became a slave trader.

Guzmán's activities depopulated the region, and most of the governors who followed did so little to improve the situation that the Franciscan missionaries returning from Tamaulipas asserted that the Spanish governors were a worse menace than the Chichimecs themselves.

The encomiendas which had theoretically disappeared from New Spain by the 1650's surfaced in Tamaulipas under the name of *congregas*, congregations of Indians held under exactly the same conditions as the early encomiendas. The congregas became slave markets and clearing centers. The missionaries denounced the situation repeatedly with little effect. No new conquistadors could be persuaded to risk their capital in an unhealthy climate where no worthwhile mines had ever been found. The necessary stimulus finally came from the outside in the guise of the French sorties from the Louisiana territory into Texas. At the same time, English vessels made tentative landings along the Gulf coast. Such obvious threats moved the government of New Spain to take action. The coast between Pánuco and Corpus Christi was an open invitation to privateers. It had to be fortified and colonized at once.

José de Escandón (1700-1770)

When the bidding opened for the colonization charter, an army captain by the name of José de Escandón won hands down. Escandón finally settled in Querétaro where he soon foresaw the imminent need to colonize Tamaulipas. Having wide experience and a methodical mind, he proceeded to explore the country at his own expense. Knowing the terrain well, his bid, abundantly documented and presenting practicable solutions, was immediately accepted. In 1748 he received the charter to establish the province of New Santander in the lands of Tamaulipas.

Escandón established experimental farms and irrigation systems around his presidio-villages. The network of roads and bridges he developed between the twenty-two permanent settlements he left at his death served as the base for the network of modern communications.

The Internal Provinces

During the Bourbon reorganization of New Spain, José de Gálvez visited these northern provinces and declared them too remote to be centrally governed as intendancies. He therefore proposed the creation of a self-governing General Military Command for those provinces which are now the states on either side of our northern border. These so-called Internal Provinces remained too unwieldy to be governed under a single command, so a few years later, in 1787, they were split into the Internal Provinces of the East and of the West. Despite various later modifications, these are the historical designations by which they are best known during the period between 1776 and 1810.

When the War of Independence began, the Internal Provinces of the East comprised what must have been the original Nuevo Reino de León under Luis de Carvajal's royal charter of 1579: Tamaulipas, Nuevo León, Coahuila and Texas. When the 1824 Constitution gave shape to our first federal republic, the Internal Provinces disappeared and were replaced by the federal states of Tamaulipas, Nuevo León and Coahuila-Texas.

Independent Mexico

The north-east conformed to the general pattern of Mexico's nineteenth-century history as outlined earlier in this book. The unremitting Indian wars frequently reached genocidal dimensions. The centrifugal force generated by the struggle between the centralists and the federalists permanently lost us Texas, New Mexico and Upper California and almost lost us the Yucatán peninsula as well. A picturesque despot by the name of Santiago Vidaurri emerged in Monterrey and dominated Nuevo León politics for a time. He was a military bully in the style of Santa Anna and fully matched his prototype in ideological inconsistency. When his star was rising, he annexed Coahuila to Nuevo León and even encouraged talk of secession and a new Republic of the Sierra Madre. Starting out as a fanatical liberal at the time of the 1856 Constitution, his frictions with Juárez made an imperialist of him. He refused to hand over the customs revenues to the hard-pressed republic during the French invasion and Juárez decided to cut him down to size by decreeing the separation of Coahuila from Nuevo León. A plebiscite was held to allow the people of Nuevo León to choose between Juárez and the liberal republic on the one hand, and Vidaurri and Maximilian on the other. Vidaurri lost, left the country, but soon after returned to become Imperial Counselor and then Maximilian's Secretary of the Imperial Treasury.

After the fall of the Empire, Vidaurri was captured and shot as a traitor by Porfirio Díaz. So runs, alas, most of our political history during that hopelessly benighted century.

The economic development of the northern cities traces the country's general development far better than the minutely detailed accounts of military movements and political intrigues that all too often pass for history. A glance at Torréon (Coahuila), Tampico (Tamaulipas) and Monterrey during the century and a half following Independence should suffice to make our point.

Torréon

In 1825, the London banking firm Baring Brothers bought the assets of the then bankrupt Marquesado de San Miguel de Aguayo in northern Mexico. The assets consisted mainly of vast tracts of land and sheep haciendas in the state of Coahuila. They included on their western boundary lines, adjoining Durango, the fertile land of the Nazas River valley, an area called La Laguna where the city of Torréon would suddenly and surprisingly sprout a few decades later.

Baring Brothers had let itself get carried away by the enthusiasm that Mexican independence from Spain generated in London. The mines, the lands were now there for the taking; one such venture was the Baring Brothers' purchase of the Marquesado. It had been the largest and richest latifundio in Mexico for close to two hundred years. Its founder was Francisco de Urdiñola, who acquired great holdings in Coahuila, setting up his headquarters in the hacienda of Patos, which he founded. His extensive plantings of vineyards throughout the temperate second-storey valleys of New Vizcaya laid the foundation for the region's thriving modern wine industry.

Baring Brothers found its Mexican venture ultimately unrewarding and, like the Real del Monte investors, gave up too soon, thereby losing properties that were soon to become among the most prosperous enterprises ever to flourish on Mexican soil. In 1840, Baring Brothers sold out to the Sánchez Navarro brothers, Jacobo and Carlos, two energetic hacendados whose family had accumulated a sizable latifundio in the course of the previous century. With the acquisition of the Marquesado lands, their consolidated haciendas constituted the largest privately held estate in the entire American continent. On the map, they covered a large part of the state of Coahuila, half the size of England – 16.6 million acres against England's 32.5 million. The Sánchez Navarro latifundio is, by its very size, the exemplar of the extensive cattle operation typical of the northern hacienda, as opposed to the smaller, though still very large southern haciendas devoted to intensive agriculture. This economic empire did not last long: it collapsed along with Maximilian's. It failed for political reasons, though, not because of indifferent management or absentee ownership. On the contrary, their management was exceptionally efficient, hard-headed and commercial in outlook, as opposed to that of many capitalists who acquired haciendas as status symbols.

Meanwhile, Torréon grew unnoticed in the background of these great happenings. The payments due to Baring Brothers and the financial crunch brought about by the war with the U.S. obliged the Sánchez Navarros to sell off two of their estates in 1848, the very profitable wine and brandy Hacienda del Rosario in Parras, and the enormous but utterly unprofitable and remote Chichimec-infested Hacienda de San Lorenzo de La Laguna, in the furthest south-west corner of their latifundio. The sale thus left them with surplus cash for working capital and a clean title to an estate that, though diminished, still dwarfed the neighboring haciendas with its 15 million acres.

The man who bought La Laguna immediately started an ambitious irrigation

project of the Nazas River, which ran through the property, and Torréon takes its
name from a tower at one end of the project's ramparts.

Torréon was little more than a name until the building of the railroad from
Mexico City to Ciudad Juárez and El Paso. A foresighted real-estate man had
subdivided all the land around the future railroad station and its arrival in 1888
turned his subdivision into the future city of Torréon. In 1902, the Coahuila-Pacific
line joined Torréon to Saltillo, and it became the third most important railroad town
in Mexico. Its inhabitants, a thrifty and creative race of farmers and *macehuals*, have
since made Torréon the crucial distribution center of north-western Mexico.

Tampico

Boom towns and ghost towns attend every mineral bonanza, whether the result
of silver, gold, uranium or oil strikes. Tampico, now a fairly prosperous port on the
Gulf, encloses in its economic fabric the ghost of a boom town whose per capita
wealth was the highest in Mexico during the years of the Revolution and the First
World War. Founded in 1828, Tampico made little mark on the regional economy
until 1898, when the Pierce Oil Company built a refinery there for imported crude
oils. The discovery of the *Faja de Oro* (Golden Strip) oilfields, in northern Veracruz,
combined with the onset of the First World War, made Tampico, with its refining
and port capacity, briefly the oilshipping capital of the world. The town boomed right
through the Mexican Revolution and the European war, despite the 1914 landing of
the American marines. While the rest of the country sank into a bog of
unproductiveness and every local *caudillo* printed his own money (*bilimbiques*) by the
carload, in Tampico, gold and silver coins were the common currency.

The seepage of salt water into the Faja de Oro oilwells brought Tampico's boom
to an end in the early twenties. It had lasted long enough to leave a valuable and
workable infrastructure of roads and port facilities which facilitated the development
of the hinterland and provided a ready market for its crops and livestock. The point of
Tampico's story is simply that mineral wealth brings only transitory plenty, whereas
lasting prosperity depends on an entirely different kind of economic activity – that
which created new wealth rather than simply extracting buried treasure from the
earth. Tampico's prosperity outlived its boom years because a sufficient proportion of
that treasure was transformed into productive capital.

Monterrey

Nature was not kind to Monterrey. Or rather, it was not generous, which, in the
final tally, amounted to being most kind.

The valley's magnificence could not disguise the fact that the countryside was
practically a desert, with bitter winters and summers like a furnace. Its richest mine,
La Iguana, raised brief hopes in the 1750's then petered out in less than ten years.
Their hostile environment forced the reineros to adapt themselves to adversity by
developing the puritanical work ethic that paid off so richly in the end. They put their
capital to work when all the treasure of Mexico's mines had already been spent on
inglorious and useless wars or on glorious and still useful buildings.

The American Civil War brought Monterrey its first substantial influx of capital.
The Union blockade of Confederate ports obliged the southern cotton growers to
ship their crops overland to Monterrey and thence to England via Matamoros. Many
of Monterrey's founding fortunes date from this period and had their origin in this
windfall.

The defeat of the Confederacy brought Monterrey's prosperity to an end as
sudden as its beginning. The railroads, which had made Torréon rich, deprived

Monterrey of its importance as a commercial entrepot. Merchants now bought directly from the producers and manufacturers. The nature of that depression showed the Monterrey capitalists the way out: they became producers and manufacturers themselves. They had made easy money as middlemen during the Civil War, but they saw that industrial production – especially the production of capital rather than consumer goods – would bring them a more lasting prosperity. Thus Monterrey became the industrial capital of the country around the turn of the century.

Monterrey has now slipped from its premier industrial position in the country for political and demographic, rather than technical, reasons. No city can compete in any activity with the immense amount of power, wealth and talent concentrated in Mexico City. Faced with such competition, Monterrey has taken a back seat, though not its entrepreneurs. They have merely moved large chunks of capital into the DF and built new factories there so that despite grave body blows – including the probably political assassination of the patriarch of the Monterrey oligarchy during the Echeverría regime – and despite recent financial scandals involving stock market manipulation, the Monterrey "group" still carries a lot of clout in the Mexican economy.

The fact that Monterrey became rich without silver mines, haciendas or oil wells irked the majority of lottery-minded Mexicans. They attributed Monterrey's success solely to the avarice of its inhabitants. Nothing is further from the truth. Regiomontanos practice systematic thrift because they know the cost and value of money. They do not amass wealth for its own sake, the earmark of avarice, but put it to use in the creation of new industries. This, and other old-fashioned virtues, have given the citizenry of Monterrey an authority that has challenged and withstood the impositions of Mexico's most insolent and domineering regimes.

The States of Baja California and Baja California Sur, Chihuahua, Sonora, Sinaloa

Sinaloa and Baja California Sur are not border states, but they are most definitely frontier states and have been so since long before the arrival of the Spaniards. The frontier does not necessarily coincide with the border between the two countries. Its character is psychological rather than geographical. It represents the always precarious equilibrium between the impulse to expand and the incapacity to do so.

We have already seen how the U.S.-Mexico border reached its present physical conformation. The frontier is something else, and both Sinaloa and Baja California Sur are good examples of non-border frontiers. Culiacán (the capital of Sinaloa), for instance, was for a long time the northernmost frontier of Mesoamerica, placed at the tip of a cultural peninsula that extended northward into the stormy lands of the nomadic Chichimecs. Culiacán was an independent seigniory at the time of the Conquest.

The Spanish town of Culiacán was founded in 1531 by Nuño de Guzmán. For a long time after its founding the Spanish city remained as isolated as the Mesoamerican had been, and in every sense the northernmost frontier of New Spain. In fact, after Nuño de Guzmán's imprisonment, even the Spanish authorities seemed to have forgotten about it. Even Francisco de Ibarra, the most illustrious of the second wave of conquistadors had no idea that it existed. When he marched out of Zacatecas, a precocious sixteen-year-old heading an almost equally youthful army, he skirted the Sierra Madre in a north-westerly direction discovering silver mines and founding cities as he went. From Durango, his explorations branched north to Chihuahua and west toward Sinaloa.

One of his men registered the first of the silver mines in southern Chihuahua.

Unimportant as they seemed in comparison with the great *reales* of central Mexico, these mines tapped the northern end of the geological strata known as the Zacatecas "silver belt," and led to other discoveries which have made present day Chihuahua Mexico's principal silver producing state.

Even then, however, they attracted the population necessary to keep the Indians at bay and start the haciendas needed to supply the mines with food and livestock. Cattle thrived in those virgin prairies and eventually the cattle barons became as rich as the miners and politically far more important. Surrounded on all sides by the vast Comanche-ridden plains, the cattlemen armed their cowboys – *vaqueros* – and organized militias which made them the strong men of the region. The mine-convent-hacienda formula that describes Mexico's heartland breaks down in the immensity of Chihuahua and the rest of the northern frontier states. They are too big, the mines too few and far between. This area developed along the line of the cattle ranch-mission-presidio colonization, which left great empty spaces open to foreign invasions.

When Ibarra descended from the high sierra to the torrid plains on the Pacific coast, instead of finding the wilderness and the savage Indians he expected, he came across the Spanish encomendero town of Culiacán whose existence he had not been aware of. One of the more prosperous encomenderos talked him into marching north against the Yaquis of Sonora, who in 1533 had trounced and repulsed the first Spanish expeditionary force.

Undaunted by the stories of the Yaquis' prowess as warriors, he proceeded to the heart of their country, a region then known as Ostimuri, between the Yaqui and the Mayo Rivers. There he astonished his companions by approaching the Yaquis peaceably, speaking to them in a friendly fashion and, more astonishing still, being similarly received by them.

After this foray into Sonora, he returned to Sinaloa, going as far south as Chametla. In the hills behind Mazatlán – a town still very much in the future – he founded the Villa de San Sebastian de la Concordia and the mining towns of Copala and Pánuco, where he died in 1575.

Culiacán remained the northern frontier post until the arrival of the Jesuits in 1591. Finding most of New Spain and its various sub-kingdoms preempted by the mendicant orders, the Jesuits directed their missionary efforts toward the north-western frontier. The nomadic Indians of the north only knew the Spaniards as warriors, predators and despoilers of their land. Their hatred for the newcomers was richly deserved. The missionaries thus had to spend the following two hundred years trying to erase that first impression. The missionary martyrs of the northern territories far outnumber those of the south. In spite of such bitter hostility, the Jesuits, like the Franciscans in the north-east, ended by winning over the Indians. After founding their first mission in Culiacán in 1591, they founded others throughout western Chihuahua, Sinaloa, Sonora, Arizona, New Mexico and, a hundred years later, the Baja California peninsula.

The success of the Jesuits' missions depended now on keeping the Spaniard, rather than the Indian, at bay. Since the Spaniards wanted the Indians for slave labor and the Jesuits were determined to protect them according to the laws of their Order and of the Spanish Crown, the moment Spaniards appeared on the horizon the missionaries sent the Indians off into the hills, presumably to tend their corn *milpas*, scattered their flocks and met the Spaniards with what seemed to be a recently abandoned mission.

Of all the vast and empty provinces of the north-west, the emptiest and most desolate were the Californias. The more energetic Indians had always shunned the long, bony-shanked peninsula in favor of the mainland route toward the Mesoamerican south. The austere beauty of its deserts and mountains impressed neither the southward bound Indians nor the northward bound Spaniards. Numerous expeditions bound for the Californias set out in the course of the sixteenth and seventeenth centuries. They surveyed and mapped the coastline in great detail, but one look into the dismal desert of the hinterland sent them scurrying back to their boats. The natives, now mostly extinct, were too abjectly poor and primitive to be even considered ignorant. They had no tools or vessels of any kind, built no shelters, and fed on prickly pears and later on the sundried prickly pear seeds extracted from their own droppings. They ate spiders, snakes, scorpions, maggots . . . anything small that moved. Their only weapons were darts and a small, curved stick they hurled like a boomerang.

The first expedition to venture inland left San Blas in 1678. A singularly gifted and purposeful Italian Jesuit by the name of Chini — remembered in Mexico as Father Kino — accompanied the expedition as Royal Cartographer. Though he was later immensely successful as an explorer and colonizer of Sonora and Arizona, Baja California utterly defeated him. A skirmish with the Indians in La Paz and the disappearance of a soldier discouraged further exploration. Given the miserliness of the land and the abject condition of the natives, the early Jesuit missions in Baja California may perhaps be the only ones in the world to which no selfish purpose can be imputed.

Today

The building of the trans-peninsular highway coincided with the world-wide diaspora of the hippies, many of whom took their drugdreams to the solitudinous stretches of the Baja California desert. In any case they did not affect the touristic poles of the peninsula: in the north the honky-tonk machine of Tijuana, across the border from San Diego, and in the south, the luxurious seclusion of clubs and resort hotels of Cabo San Lucas and other nearby coves, capes and islands. This southern tourist strip is the rich man's Baja — as opposed to Tijuana, which defies description. The frequenters of these posh resorts are not really tourists, though, nor even "travelers" in the accepted sense of the word. They are generally well-heeled sportsmen to whom the trans-peninsular highway means nothing since they habitually fly their own planes or sail their own boats to whichever destination they choose. To them, the previous lack of communication meant a very welcome seclusion in what still seemed virgin territory with incomparable fishing. It held, in other words, the attraction of the frontier and the wilderness, but without inconvenient isolation — landing strips and marinas dot the coast — and the very best plumbing money can buy.

Across the Gulf of California — or Sea of Cortés — Sonora and Sinaloa have taken an entirely different tack. Their tourism is of the modern nomadic sort, with endless trailer caravans and crowded trailer parks. Mazatlán, straight across the Gulf from the tip of Baja California is one of their big stops. Tourism is more important to Mazatlán than to any other town in these two big agricultural states — except perhaps the beautiful colonial city of Alamos in Sonora — yet the local authorities have allowed the old town to rot. Mazatlán's charm resided in the stylistic consistency of the houses along its waterfront and downtown city blocks all built in a rather wayward Neo-Classical style of iron-grilled French windows and giant *zaguanes* (coach doors) topped by substantial cornices, and opening into surrounding luminous interiors of airy corridors and high ceilings with fretted borders — an architectural portrait of the substantial German, Spanish and French merchants who built the town during the

latter half of the nineteenth century. Of the better known tourist resorts, only Mazatlán fully represented this period, which in one or two generations will acquire the special significance that the late nineteenth century had for those of us born in the first half of the twentieth – perhaps a triumph of nostalgia over elegance, but the sentiment is real.

Today it is the tragic example of a town whose charm has been destroyed by the stranglehold of a few powerful landlords, who have instead preferred to build countless highrise condominiums and hotels along the splendid beaches north of Mazatlán. The jungle of ficus roots lurking underground, waiting to take over and sprouting out of every crack in the sidewalk, has invaded the roofless shells of tall-windowed row houses, strangler figs buttressing their walls against hurricanes, their aerial roots dropping from branches to practice their Gaudí arabesques on the crumbling walls and cornices, following nature's obligation to imitate art. Through a failure in distributive justice – and a lack of respect for the community's feelings – Mazatlán has become a congery of haunted houses, a ghost town haunted by its long-suffering inhabitants.

Heads or Tails, Eagle or Sun

In Mexico, when you flip a coin you do not say "Heads or tails'" but "*Aguila o sol?*" – eagle or sun – the two sides of all our old coins. The eagle was the Aztec glyph for the sun, but it was also the devourer of human hearts that decorates our national emblem and without which the sun would not rise on the morrow. Does it mean anything that the sun has disappeared from the modern Mexican coins but not the eagle?

In Sonora and Sinaloa we can see the flipping of the coin. Arbitrarily split up into two separate states in 1830, they offer a dramatic example of the irresponsiblity of this system. Their economic activity – farming, fishing, cattle and poultry raising – and especially their technical approach to it, reveals the underlying unity of the region and the people. From Culiacán to Hermosillo a series of irrigation systems has made this north-western corner of Mexico a farming emporium of prime importance. The crops change as one moves north from winter vegetables, sugar cane, tropical fruits and grains around Culiacán to wheat, cotton, orange and pecan groves around Hermosillo. The Sonora desert, with its *sahuaros* and the *piñon* covered ranges toward the east, supports large herds of cattle. All along the Mexico-U.S. border the *maquiladoras* have created hundreds of thousands of jobs producing components for American industry and their development clearly points to a possibility for the economic collaboration that must be the first step in solving the bitter problems between the two countries.

That is the sunny side of the coin. On the dark side, the eagle continues devouring human hearts while filling inhuman bank accounts with great wealth. Opium and marijuana are produced in the Sinaloa hills and smuggled by every imaginable means – including stuffed tomatoes – into the insatiable and ever growing U.S. market. Though the operation "Condor" put into effect during José López Portillo's term (1976-82) has put a stop to the terrifying streetcorner, high-noon shootouts in Culiacán and happenings like the massacre of the entire clientele of a Mazatlán seaside beer garden, the continued media campaign shows that, though subdued, the producers and the runners are still active.

The drug trade had an innocent – well, relatively innocent – beginning. Several boatloads of Chinese immigrants, rejected by immigration authorities in California, landed in Mazatlán in the 1890's, and from there spread northward into Sonora with the hope of reaching their families in the U.S. They had brought seeds with them and planted the poppy for their own use. It was a matter openly discussed early in the century — poppies grew in parterres in the municipal gardens and in private houses — but what the Chinese did with them was their own business. World War II changed all that. The Axis takeover of Turkey's opium fields left the Allies without a source of morphine. Knowing the poppy thrived in Sinaloa, the U.S. and Mexico by mutual consent financed the massive production of opium, and Sinaloa became the chief supplier of the drug for the Allied powers.

It was ingenuous to assume production would stop at the end of the war. Or perhaps disingenuous, since many latter-day political fortunes are reputably derived from the industry. Certainly the hill farmers who had learned the business had no intention of giving up such a lottery-prize of a crop, and when it ceased being ethical, organized crime took over. The pleas of presidential candidates to the people of this region that they return to planting corn and beans "so their children can hold their heads high" must produce more amazement than mockery. After all, they were asking people used to making several millions in one brief haul to return to the backbreaking life of hard scrabble farming.

If we flip the coin to *sol* once more, though, we find in the southernmost littoral of Sinaloa a stretch of beaches, lagoons, estuaries and off-shore islands between Mazatlán and Teacapán, what may be in a tourist-thronged world the last refuge of the Noble Savage. That may be where the future lies for lovers of nature and secluded villages with modern plumbing. The year has two seasons here, a hot, humid, buggy summer from the middle of June to the middle of October and, for the rest of the year, a season of heavenly transparency, mildness and buglessness that may constitute the longest-lasting spring on earth. The long off-shore islands are permanently green, subtropical savannas, where abundant fruit and grain crops grow without irrigation. In the back yards of the thatched-roofed houses flourish lush growths of mangoes, lichees, coconuts, custard apples and sourops.

The village of Teacapán, for example (Náhuatl, "wild reeds on water") whose very name describes its location on a bamboo-lined lagoon, is smack in the heart of the great oyster mother lode that stretches from Guaymas, in Sonora, to San Blas, in Nayarit. The oysters grow like crusts of barnacles in the roots of the mangrove forests that line the estuaries, as delicate and plump as the finest Bluepoints and Marennes. In June, you dive for scallops and pick bucketsful of miniature orange sand clams. Tiny estuary shrimp appear mysteriously in drainage ditches and waterholes during the rainy season. Red snappers cavort in the lagoon, practically looking for a plate to land on. Guavas grow wild where greedy orioles, cardinals and blackbirds have planted them from their fencepost perches. Villagers and visitors smack their lips at the effortlessly laden board, heedless of the cries for help as the work ethic drowns in the reckless generosity of those mackerel crowded seas.

Only in such surroundings could this text of bitter love have taken shape.

Teacapán
June 1981 - April 1982

144. *Punta Chueca (Sonora). A Seri Indian musician with a local bowed instrument, wearing a wooden head-dress with a carved bird on top.*

145. *Punta Chueca (Sonora). Seri Indian children.*

146. *The Sonora desert; on the hill to the left, a small votive chapel. An Italian Jesuit cartographer named Chini, known as Father Kino in Mexico, explored and helped colonize Sonora.*

147. *Vicam (Sonora). Cemetery of the Yaqui Indians. Vicam is one of the eight traditional Yaqui pueblos, where the councils of administration meet.*

148. *Vicam (Sonora). Yaqui Indian girl eating a* tamal. *On* All Souls Day *the Mexicans visit the cemeteries to eat and drink until late into the night.*

147

148

221

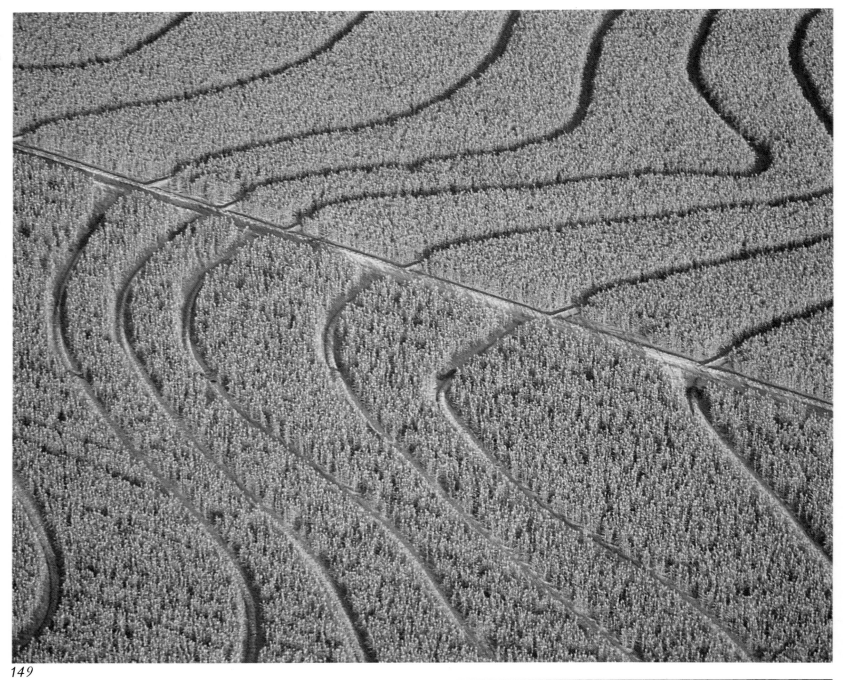

149

150

51

52

149. *Aerial view of the rice fields in Sinaloa.*

150. *San Xavier (Baja California). Bell tower of the mission house, in an oasis in the desert.*

151. *Near San Quintin (Baja California). Workers in the tomato fields.*

152. *Culiacán (Sinaloa). Sinaloan peasant woman with hat and headscarves to protect her from the mosquitoes and chemicals and the sun.*

153. *Sinaloan peasant women dressed to work in winter vegetable farms. Head kerchiefs are purely utilitarian, as a defense against gnats and mosquitoes, and trousers tied at the ankles are worn under the dress for the same reason. Younger women frequently add a wild sunflower to the hat.*

154

154. *Aerial view of the coast of Sinaloa. River estuaries, lagoons and the open sea frequently merge around the sandy strands and the long strips of mangroves in whose roots oysters lodge.*

155. *The long* tapos, *fence-like shrimp traps in the estuaries of southern Sinaloa.*

156. *Near Mexicali (Baja California). The northern shore of the great salt lake. Mexicali, like Calexico, its twin city on the U.S. side of the border, is a made-up name derived from Mexico and California.*

157. *Punta Chueca (Sonora). Young Indian girl of the Seri tribe walking on the coast.*

158. *Tenejapa (Chiapas). Indian standing in front of the wall of a church, which is decorated with the branches of trees. Men dressed like this form part of the organizing group for local festivities, where they are in charge of the drinks and other activities.*

159-163. *Mexican faces.*

164. *Sahuayo (Michoacán). Church facade.*

165. *Uxmal (Yucatán). This Indian textile surrounds a Spanish Madonna carved by native hands. It is to be found near the reception desk in the main hotel in Uxmal and seems to sum up the folk heritage of modern Mexico.*

166. *Teposcolula (Oaxaca). Life-size wooden polychrome statues in the Dominican monastery.*

165

166

167

168

169

234

170

171

167. *Decorative grille protecting window, and painted wall.*

168. *Mérida (Yucatán). Naive wall-painting in a bar.*

169. *Progreso (Yucatán). Wall-painting in the market.*

170. *Mérida (Yucatán). Hand prints traditionally placed on walls suggest the prehistoric hands scrawled on the walls of caves.*

171. *Valladolid (Yucatán). Painting on a street wall.*

173

172. *Monterrey (Nuevo León).*
Aerial view of a modern housing development.

173. *Coatzacoalcos (Veracruz). The glint of a*
setting sun on an oil refinery against a stormy
sky.

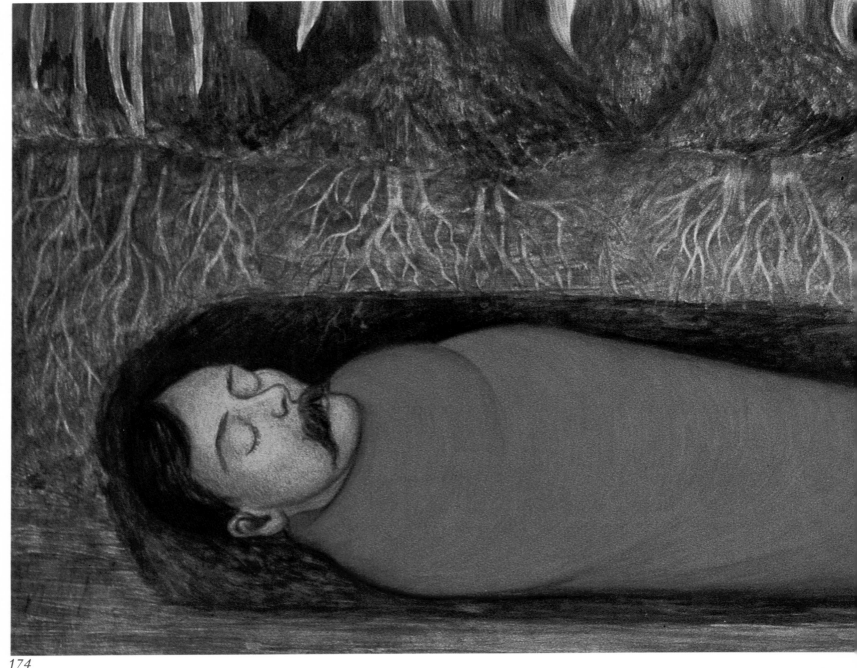

174

174. Chapingo (State of Mexico). A panel showing the dead Zapata: one of the murals of Diego Rivera's masterpiece, which Mexicans refer to as their Sistine Chapel.

175. Mexico City. Escuela de Maestros; a mural by José Clemente Orozco, 1947.

175

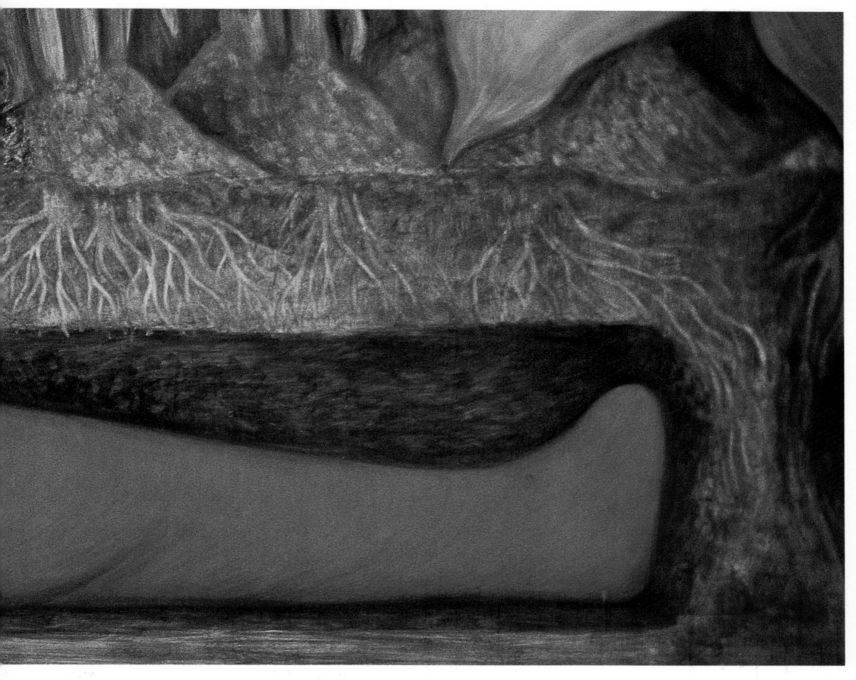

176. *Guadalajara. Palacio de Gobierno. José Clemente Orozco's mural showing Miguel Hidalgo y Costilla, the priest who initiated the War of Independence.*

239

Chronology

1200-300 BC	Olmec domination
100-900 AD	Teotihuacán domination
900-1300 AD	Toltec domination
1325-1521	Mexica-Aztec domination
1517	First recorded sighting of what is now Mexico
1518	Expedition of Juan de Grijalva
18 November 1518	Cortés sails from Cuba with 11 ships, 508 soldiers and captains, 100 seamen, 16 horses, 10 bronze guns and 13 shotguns
12 March 1519	Cortés lands in what is now Tabasco
Good Friday 1519	Cortés founds Veracruz
13 August 1521	Conquest of Mexico
1524	Arrival of first Franciscans
1527	First Audiencia under Nuño de Guzmán
1528	Zumárraga named first bishop of what is now Mexico City
1529	Cortés named Captain General and Marquess of the Valley of Oaxaca
1531	First apparition of the Virgin of Guadalupe
January 1531	Second Audiencia
1535-50	First Viceroy Mendoza's administration. Exploration of northern territories and efforts to suppress encomienda system
1542	New Laws promulgated by Spanish Crown
1548	First silver strike in Zacatecas
1550	Luis Velasco succeeds Mendoza as Viceroy
1552	Silver strike in Real del Monte
1552-1591	Chichimeca War
1554	Route to Philippines is discovered
1562	Francisco Ibarra establishes Reino de Nueva Galicia
1566	Aborted coup of Martín Cortés
1571	Inquisition established
1571	Manila Galleon begins voyages from Spain to the Orient via Mexico
1572	Jesuits transferred from Florida to Mexico
1579	Philip II's grant to Carvajal of territory now Coahuila, Nuevo León, Texas and Tamaulipas
1591	All lands in Mexico declared property of the Spanish Crown
1602	Rebellion of slaves under Yanga
1621	Viceroy de Gelves's administration marked by mounting conflict between Church and State with de Gelves excommunicated by Archbishop Serna and Mexico under interdict
1722-34	Casafuerte Viceroy
1767	Jesuits expelled from Spain and all her dominions
1770's	José de Galvez organizes Internal Provinces
1789-94	Viceroy Revillagigedo's administration high point in Spanish rule
16 September 1810	Hidalgo's "Grito de Dolores" calls for independence from Spain
1811	Insurgents defeated and Hidalgo executed
1813	Morelos calls First Constitutional Assembly
1815	Morelos captured and executed
1815	Tabasco secedes from Mexico, returns in 1821
1821	Iturbide signs Plan de Iguala 24 February and enters Mexico City 27 September as Emperor
1823	Iturbide abdicates
1824-34	First Federalist regime, Guadalupe Victoria first president
1835-46	Centralist interregnum
1838-48	Yucatán War of the Castes
1839	Yucatán secedes from Mexico
1846	Restoration of Federalism
1846-48	War with the United States (see detailed chronology in chapter 5)
1857	Constitution
1857	Reform Laws signed
1858-61	Reform Wars
1861	European intervention
12 June 1864	Maximilian enters Mexico City as Emperor
15 May 1867	Maximilian defeated and captured at Querétaro
19 June 1867	Maximilian executed
1867	Benito Juárez elected president
18 July 1867	Death of Juárez
Good Friday 1868	Crucifixion of Chebched boy begins Chiapas War of the Castes
1906-07	Strikes at the Cananea Consolidated Copper Company and at the textile mill in Río Blanco
20 November 1910	Aquiles Serdán, his sister Carmen and brother Máximo fire first shots of Revolution
25 May 1911	Díaz resigns as president
6 November 1911	Madero inaugurated as president
19 February 1913	Madero forced to resign, three days later he is executed
February 1913	Huerta seizes power
14 July 1914	Huerta forced to resign
1917	Constitution
1919	Zapata assassinated
1920	Carranza assassinated
1920-24	Obregón Presidency
1923	Pancho Villa assassinated
1924-28	Calles Presidency
1926-29	Cristero Rebellion
1929	Plutarco Elías Calles founds the National Revolutionary Party

Glossary

agave	a genus of plants which includes the American Aloe, and also the species *henequén* and *maguey* (qq.v.)
amate	the white wild fig tree (*Ficus albus*)
Anáhuac	"place between two waters," a name applied to the valley surrounding Tenochtitlán specifically, and to the Aztec Empire generally.
Audiencia	the supreme tribunal, originally set up by the Spanish Crown to limit the power of the conquistadors, which governed in New Spain in conjunction with the Viceroy
barranca	a deep gorge
barrio	a neighborhood, or quarter in a city
bilimbique	Revolutionary paper money whose name traditionally derives from the name of William Vique, the cashier of an American mining company whose signed vouchers served as local currency.
cachito	literally "a little piece," used to denote the twentieth part of a full lottery ticket
cacique	a native chieftain (orig. Caribbean)
calpuli	the quarters into which Aztec cities were divided
calpulalli	the common lands held by the *calpuli* (q.v.)
caribal	the minimal forest dwelling of the Lacandones
casco	the total building complex of a *hacienda* (q.v.), usually enclosed by high walls
charro	the Mexican cowboy
chía water	any fresh fruit drink (usually lemonade) in which the seeds of the chía plant (sage) have been soaked, producing a mucilaginous effect
chicle	the latex from which chewing-gum is made
Churrigueresque	a florid Baroque style of architecture originated by the Churriguera family in Spain
comunidades	the Indian communities
congregas	the latter day *encomiendas* (q.v.)
corregimiento	the Crown version of the feudal *encomienda* (q.v.)
Creole	a pure-blooded European (generally Spanish) born in Spanish America
ejido	a system of common land tenure ("social property") based on usufruct rather than outright ownership
ejidatorio	beneficiary of the *ejido* (q.v.)
encomienda	a group of native populations and their lands held in trust by a conquistador and his descendants
encomendero	beneficiary of the *encomienda* (q.v.)
entheogenic	("God-within-us"), adjective coined by Gordon Wasson, the renowned student of mycology, to describe all hallucinogenic mushrooms
frijoles	Mexican beans, a staple item of Mexican diet
gachupín	a Spanish immigrant
hacienda	a self-sufficient, privately owned farm with resident management. Haciendas ranged in size from a few hundred hectares to several million
hacendado	the owner of a *hacienda* (q.v.)
henequén	the plant from which sisal is made
hidalgo	a member of the Spanish gentry
ingenio	a sugar mill
jarocho	a native of Veracruz
latifundista	the owner of a large estate, more specifically one exceeding the legal property limitations
macehual	a peasant in Náhuatl-speaking populations
maguey	the plant from which *pulque* (q.v.) is extracted
malinchismo	the servile adoption of foreign values and customs in preference to their native counterparts, regardless of their merits
maquiladora	a company providing labor-intensive services to foreign industry
marías	Indian women, mainly Otomí-speaking Mazatecas, who flock to Mexico City from the nearby sierras in search of a livelihood
mesta	a migratory sheep walk, generally that from the lowlands of Querétaro and Guanajuato to the pastures of the northern states
mestizo	of mixed blood (usually Spanish and Indian)
mexica	the original stock from which the Aztecs sprang. Not to be confused with "Mexico" or "Mexican" in the modern sense

milpa	a maize patch
mudéjar	in the Moorish style
Náhuatl	the language of the *Mexicas* (q.v.) and related peoples
obrajes	textile mills in colonial times
Occidente	a general term used to designate the culture of the western states (Michoacán, Colima, Jalisco, Nayarit)
pachocha	money, "pile" (a corruption of Pachuca, the name of a town famous for its silver mines)
Purépecha	the dominant people of Michoacán at the time of the Conquest, called "Tarascos" by the Spaniards
peninsular	of or pertaining to the Iberian peninsula and its people
piñata	a decorated earthenware pot filled with goodies and whacked open with a stick at children's parties
piñón	the edible seed of the pine cone
Plateresque	a Spanish Renaissance architectural style, derived from the decorative motifs of the Spanish silversmiths (*plateros*)
poblano	of or pertaining to the city of Puebla
presidio	a garrison town, usually one of the many along the routes to the mines
pueblo	the word used in Mexican history to refer to exclusively Indian communities
pulque	the fermented juice of the *maguey* (q.v.)
quinta	a country house
real	a mine
regiomontano	a native of Monterrey
reinero	the colonial designation for a native of the Nuevo Reino de León in general, and of its principal city of Monterrey in particular
retablo	the reredos of an altar
sahuaro	a strikingly dramatic organ cactus found in the Sonora desert
seigniory	a feudal domain
simpatía	sympathy in the sense of charm and instinctive attraction, mostly used in the adjectival forms *simpatico* or *simpatica*
taco	a maize *tortilla* (q.v.) wrapped around anything eatable
tamemes	pre-Hispanic Indian porters
tapatio	of or pertaining to the people of Jalisco
Tarasco	see Purépecha
-tepec	word-ending indicating an inhabited hill (e.g. Chapultepec)
-tépetl	word-ending indicating an uninhabited hill (e.g. Popocatépetl)
tertulia	a literary circle
teules	"demons," applied to the original conquistadors by the awe-struck Indians who first beheld them
tienda de raya	a company store, which became the means of keeping the peons in serfdom through debt
tortilla	a thin maize pancake, the outside of a *taco* (q.v.)
yucateco	a native of Yucatán
zaguanes	the coach entrances to large houses
zócalo	the central square of any large town, by analogy with the central square of Mexico City (so named)
Zona Rosa	the swinging area around the chic stores and restaurants in Mexico City

All accents in Spanish are like the French acute accent. In this text the only *grave* accent occurs in the Catalonian surname Tolsà. When no accent is indicated the emphasis always falls on the penultimate syllable, unless the word ends with a consonant other than "m", "n" or "s", in which case the last syllable is accented.

Readers may like to be reminded that the pronunciation of Spanish consonants follows roughly the same rules as English (e.g. "ch" as in "much"), with the exception of the initial "h" (which is silent, e.g. "hacienda"), "j" (which is strongly aspirated), "g" (which is aspirated before "e" and "i" but hard before "a", "o" and "u"), and "qu" which is always pronounced as "k".

243